Fundraising on the Internet

Recruiting and renewing donors online

Edited by

Nick Allen
Mal Warwick
Mal Warwick & Associates, Inc.

Michael Stein
Institute for Global Communications

D1605006

STRATHMOOR
PRESS

To order more copies of this book, contact the publisher:

Strathmoor Press, Inc.
2550 Ninth Street
Suite 1040
Berkeley, California 94710-2516
Order toll-free (800) 217-7377
E-mail info@strathmoor.com

Printed and bound in Canada. First printing, September 1996.

ISBN 0-9624891-8-2

Most of Chapters 1 and 6 first appeared in the newsletter *Successful Direct Mail & Telephone Fundraising*™ (July 1996), published by Strathmoor Press, Inc.

An earlier version of Chapter 4 appeared in the September 1995 issue of the U.K. magazine *Professional Fundraising* and the November 1995 issue of *The NonProfit Times*. The text was revised in February 1996. Reprinted with permission. Copyright © 1996 Hewitt and Johnston Consultants.

Chapter 7 is copyright © 1996 by the Support Center for Nonprofit Management. Reprinted with permission.

Chapter 8 is from *The Nonprofit Guide to the Internet* by Robbin Zeff. Copyright © 1996 John Wiley & Sons, Inc. Reprinted by permission of John Wiley & Sons, Inc.

In this book . . .

What you'll find in this book, and why you should read it

1. Nick Allen: **Who's doing what on the Internet**

2. Mal Warwick: **Anatomy of a Web site**

3. Michael Stein: **Tools you can use online**

4. Michael Johnston: **Fundraising opportunities online**

5. Mal Warwick: **What you already know about fundraising online!**

6. Audrie Krause: **Taking the plunge into e-mail fundraising**

7. Martha Simpson: **Web sites useful for fundraisers**

8. Robbin Zeff: **Cyber-fundraising**

9. Michael Stein: **Glossary of Internet terms**

About the principal contributors to this book

About the organizations behind this book

How this book was produced

What you'll find in this book, and why you should read it

Fundraising on the Internet is a pioneer adventure. There are few experienced guides, the trails are rough and unmarked, and the technology can be as creaky as a wooden wagon wheel.

Because fundraising on the Internet is so new, this book is necessarily a work in progress. We hope it provides a provisional map—and that you'll help us fill in some of the uncharted territory for the next edition.

Despite the uncertainties, more and more nonprofits are building World Wide Web sites and starting to prospect for gold (or at least greenbacks). A few big national organizations, such as the American Civil Liberties Union and the American Red Cross, are already bringing in significant contributions.

With near-perfect timing, the ACLU's "Keep Cyberspace Free" Web site went live the same week that President Clinton signed the Communications Decency Act, which provided for censorship of the Internet. In the site's first month, it brought in over $18,000, most from online credit card transactions. While this success represents an exceptional combination of good timing, an issue with special appeal for heavy Internet users, and the credibility of the ACLU on the censorship issue, we believe others will be able to repeat, even exceed, this success.

Already 20 or 30 million Americans have access to e-mail, online services like America Online, and the Web—and the numbers are increasing rapidly. Most college students are assigned Internet addresses when they register. Most office e-mail can send and receive messages through the Internet. And virtually every new computer includes a modem and pre-installed software for AOL or Microsoft Network (which both provide Internet access along with proprietary content).

As giving money over the Internet becomes more secure and more common, the Internet (plus AOL, etc.) could open up vast new vistas for *acquiring* new donors at reasonable costs and for *cultivating* them so they become involved and loyal members willing to continue, even increase, their financial support.

This book focuses on acquiring new donors. But we believe even greater opportunities are available right now for organizations to work with substantial numbers of their *existing* donors who are comfortable—even enthusiastic—about communicating electronically. We are already helping clients do this, and for the next edition of this book we'll have more information on what works (and, inevitably, what doesn't).

>>> In Chapter 1, Nick Allen reviews the state of the art in Internet fundraising with a report on how nonprofits are beginning to acquire new donors online—and the opportunities for establishing electronic relationships with existing donors. Nick is head of the

Internet fundraising program at Mal Warwick & Associates, a Berkeley, California-based fundraising and marketing company.

>>> Chapter 2 is entitled "Anatomy of a Web site." Here, Mal Warwick takes you screen by screen on a brief tour of one truly top-notch nonprofit site. Mal is founder and chair of Mal Warwick & Associates, co-founder and vice-chair of the Share Group telemarketing company, and author of seven previous books on fundraising.

>>> Next, in Chapter 3, Michael Stein, special projects director at the Institute for Global Communications, the nation's largest nonprofit Internet service, explains the basic technical tools of Internet fundraising.

>>> Toronto consultant Michael Johnston takes a close look at fundraising opportunities online in Chapter 4, excerpted from his forthcoming book. Mike is president of Hewitt & Johnston Consultants and has worked with hundreds of nonprofit organizations in Canada, the U.S., and the United Kingdom.

>>> In Chapter 5, Mal Warwick looks at the similarities and differences between traditional direct mail and telephone fundraising with their online analogues. He explores how some direct response techniques can be even more effective online.

>>> Audrie Krause then reports briefly on one recent success story: the significant contribution e-mail communications made to a fundraising event benefitting her organization, Computer Professionals for Social Responsibility, of which Audrie is executive director. Her case study appears as Chapter 6.

>>> Chapter 7 is a list of World Wide Web sites of special interest to fundraising professionals. The list was compiled by Martha Simpson, director of telecommunications projects at the Support Center for Nonprofit Management in San Francisco.

>>> In Chapter 8, you'll read Robbin Zeff's comments on "Cyber-Fundraising" from her forthcoming book, the *Nonprofit Guide to the Internet*, to be published in the fall of 1996 by John Wiley & Sons, Inc. Robbin is a nonprofit consultant and trainer based in Washington, D.C.

>>> Chapter 9 is Michael Stein's no-nonsense glossary of Internet terms.

In presenting all these experiences to you, are we arguing that you should rush right out onto the Internet, post an appeal for funds, and grab your share of the billions to be made there—while the getting's still good?

Of course not.

We're among the first to recognize that financial pickings online are still pretty slim for most nonprofits. There are, however, multiple reasons for a charitable cause or institution to use e-mail and the Internet—strong reasons that have little or nothing to do with fundraising.

Internal communications, for example. Program research. A platform for collaborative work. And that's just the beginning.

In many ways, fundraising and membership development are (as is so often the case) behind the curve in taking advantage of this new technology.

But how much longer do you think that's likely to be the case?

How soon will it be before usage of the Internet reaches critical mass—and "everybody" is using it as a primary source of information about the world?

And how much of a gambler are you? Are you willing to risk being left in the lurch by dramatic new fundraising opportunities online unless you venture into cyberspace now, in these pioneer days?

—Nick Allen, Michael Stein, and Mal Warwick
July 1996

>>>

1

Who's doing what on the Internet

by NICK ALLEN

How many of your donors or members have e-mail addresses?

Ten percent? One-quarter? One-half?

How many surf the World Wide Web or belong to America Online or CompuServe?

Whatever these percentages, they'll probably double by next year.

Many nonprofit organizations are starting to use their Web sites, as well as forums on AOL or CompuServe, to acquire new donors—and these efforts are beginning to pay off for some.

Far fewer groups are identifying donors who *want* to have an electronic relationship with them and then using e-mail and the Web tools to provide rich, personalized, two-way relationships. "E-members" can be educated, activated, cultivated, and even renewed in effective yet inexpensive ways impossible with the usual paper and phone contacts.

Prospecting for new donors

An organization's own World Wide Web site is the main route for online prospecting. Most organizations have a "join" button somewhere on their site, and more and more sites can accept online credit card contributions. An organization's forum on AOL or CompuServe (the two biggest online services) and the free-offer "FreeShops" on the two services are other places to attract donors. Web malls like CharitiesUSA and Canada's Charity Village also enable groups to accept contributions, but the malls have not proven effective at motivating potential donors.

For the American Civil Liberties Union, online is working. The ACLU's forum on America Online, operating since May 1995, brings in 12–15 e-mail pledges a week, plus some income from AOL usage fees.

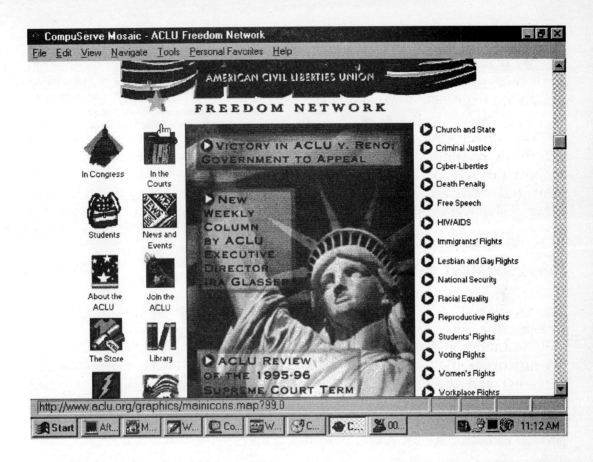

The group's big success has come from its handsome Web site, which premiered in February 1996, the same week that President Clinton signed the Communications Decency Act, hotly opposed by the Internet community. That month, the Web site—featuring a "Keep Cyberspace Free" home page—brought in $18,000 via online credit card contributions, plus some money from online "bill me" pledges paid by check. The 580 credit card donors gave a $31 average gift.

Through April (less than three months), the site had brought in $25,000 from credit cards, plus additional pledge money. The average gift remained about $31, according to online coordinator Lynn Decker. New online members are folded into the regular membership stream, but eventually a special program will be started for them.

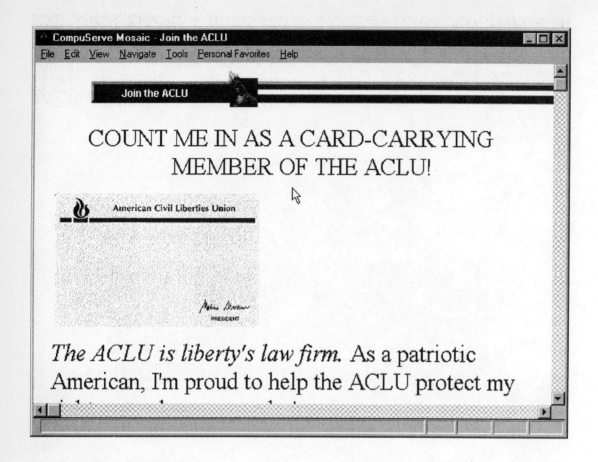

A much smaller and very different organization, the American Canoe Association, launched its Web site in April and now gets one or two new bill-me members per day (online credit cards coming soon). The premium is a free instruction manual. In addition, the association gets about 20 e-mail messages a day, ranging from information requests to messages for instructors and board members.

Rainforest Action Network's Mark Westlund says credit card contributions from its Web site "covered the initial investment of machines and staffing in the first eight months of its operation." But he cautioned that "the returns from our Web page are not astronomical. Most of our money comes through the traditional channels of direct mail, telephone, foundations, and major individual donors."

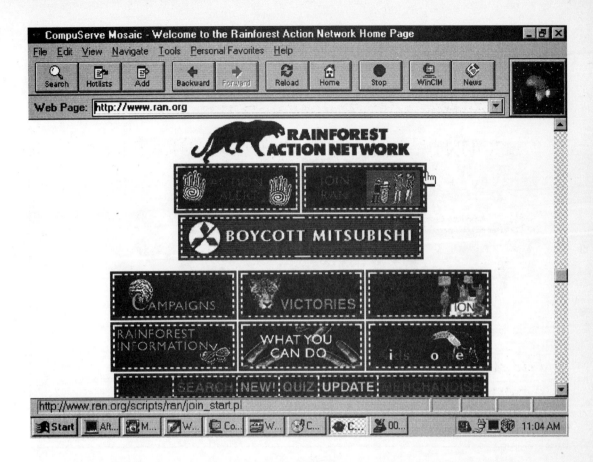

Like most other good sites, Rainforest Action Network's has many objectives other than raising money: education, activism (you can send faxes or e-mails to campaign targets right from the page), and even entertainment.

WPLN, the NPR station in Nashville, urges listeners to e-mail their pledges. The station raised over $6,000 in one week—$10,000 in a month—from e-mailed pledges. Average gift was $75; premium was a WPLN mousepad. About 40 percent of online donors are new members, says former development director Greg Pope. In addition to pledges, the station recently began to accept credit card donations online too. "We mention our Web page address, on-air, at least once each hour," says Pope. "We need to make our site a 'hot site' that people use every day so that we can lead them toward membership contributions."

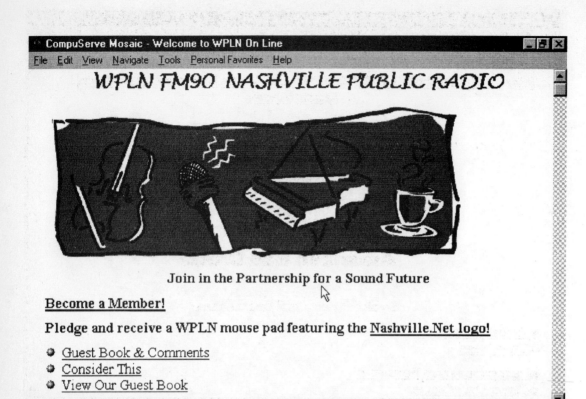

By trading advertising with a local Internet service provider, the station gets free e-mail and Web services. Since NPR and PBS audiences are educated and upscale, it's surprising that more affiliates don't make similar use of the Internet for fundraising.

The American Red Cross has been successful in getting Web contributions, especially during the kind of natural disasters it's well known for helping with. While the Red Cross has not been taking donations online, up to 30 percent of the donors calling its toll-free number, 800-HELP-NOW, say they found the number on the Web page. Internet donors average $5 more than donors from print or TV, according to Edward A. Stern of the Red Cross. And 95 percent of donors from the Web give by credit card rather than make pledges. Convincing news organizations like CNN and ABC to provide hot links from their Web sites to the Red Cross site in news stories about disasters could probably further increase donations.

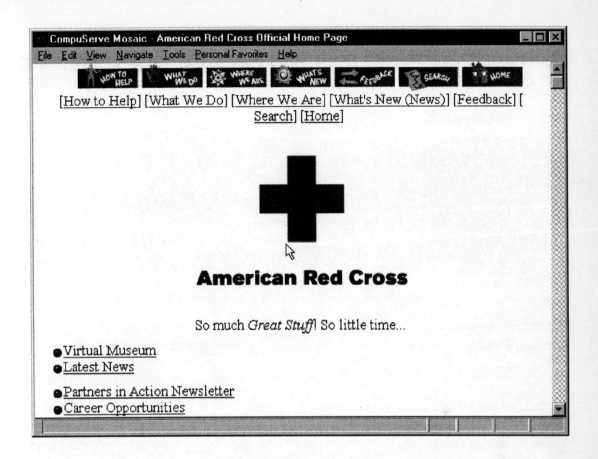

Using the online services

The National Audubon Society has advertised in the AOL FreeShop (GO FreeShop) on and off for about 18 months and brought in about 750 orders. The offer: a free trial issue of *Audubon* magazine, plus a free backpack upon payment of the $20 dues. Even though the conversion rate is low compared to other alternate source programs, the competitive advertising rate and volume of orders has nearly paid for itself, says marketing director Jennifer Doxsee.

The Nature Conservancy forum, on AOL since November 1994, has welcomed more than 1,000 new members, most at an introductory rate of $15, with a free tote bag (GO Nature). More than 50 have renewed.

The Conservancy's gorgeous new Web site offers a $25 membership with the tote bag. 46 new members signed up—and one existing member renewed online—in the site's first 10 weeks. The site gives visitors numerous opportunities to get involved. They can sign up for $25 or join the "National Leadership Circle" for $1,000 or more. They can "adopt an acre" or enlist as a volunteer. Or they can buy T-shirts and other branded merchandise. Visitors are asked to take an online survey in exchange for the free downloading of a Nature Conservancy screen saver! Asked if they may be contacted by e-mail, 90 percent say yes.

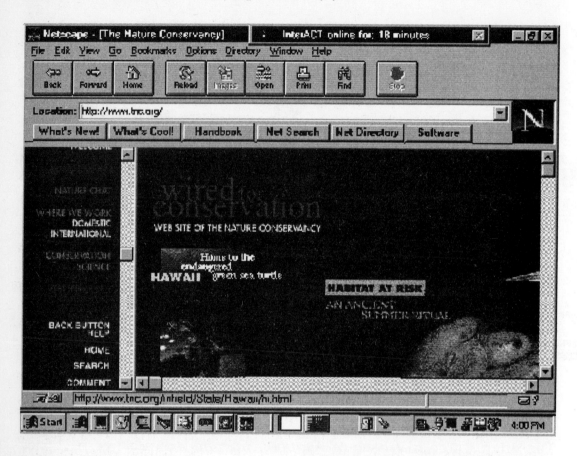

The Christian Children's Fund has been in the CompuServe mall for about two years (Go CCF) and gets about 50 responses a month. Ten of them make $21 contributions to sponsor a child for a month. The others request a sponsorship information packet. CCF welcomes the responders by e-mail, mails the package within 5 days, and phones them 15 days out. Then they enter the same membership stream as hot leads from other sources.

The FreeShop rate card lists $2,300 a month for AOL—way too pricey for nonprofit offers—but 21st Century Marketing says nonprofits usually negotiate (much) lower rates.

Online auctions

Online auctions have also reportedly raised money, though renewing these "donors" would probably require another auction. Ken Margolis Associates runs the Artrock Auction, which raised $15,000 from 100 buyers in April for the Save the Earth Foundation. The most expensive item was a signed Eagles poster, which went for $1,005. Bidders have to pay a $5 registration fee in advance, which "brings up the age of the bidders," Margolis says. The Entertainment Promotions Network says its silent online "Celebrity Internet Charity Auction" raised $4,000 for the Hollywood-based Family Assistance Program, which helps homeless families. Online bidders paid $325 for a "Seinfeld" script, the most expensive item.

Given the cost of setting up attractive home pages with photos of the items for sale and the technology to make bidding work, auctions of this size must depend on donated Internet and Web construction services. However, the economics might be different for large local or national organizations that could draw thousands of bidders for solar-powered cars, Himalayan treks, and posters of the Eagles (rock or bald).

Web sites that offer visitors the opportunity to choose among many groups for donations often seem to have trouble. The "Cookin' on the Net" Web site offered recipes from famous chefs in exchange for contributions to help poor kids get access to computers. Nonetheless, the project raised little online, despite widespread paid advertising, great free media, and big name sponsors like Microsoft. "Much of the money raised came through traditional mail as a result of the mainstream press coverage rather than through the site itself," according to Steve Glikbarg of Impact Online.

ReliefNet, which links visitors to dozens of relief organizations, has not been generating a lot of contributions in the last year, says Cliff Landesman.

In an AOL posting, Glikbarg said: "In my opinion, online fundraising is still at least a year away from being effective. . . . In the long run, I think online fundraising can be a good supplement (*not* replacement, just a supplement) for nonprofits. Don't look for thousands to come in, but it is a good way to reach new donors."

Amen!

Of course, small, local organizations can't bring in contributions like large brand-name national organizations. Most nonprofit Web sites get few or no donations, or don't even ask. Many sites don't make it easy to give. The "join" button is buried and not tied to Web pages that might motivate visitors. Even though most successful online fundraising is still small potatoes for big organizations like the ACLU or Audubon, yet their experiences demonstrate that people *will* join online. Web and AOL programs are already are paying for themselves, even if response rates are low by traditional measurements.

Things can only improve as more people use the Internet, online credit card transactions get more secure and more common, and nonprofits get more savvy about using the Internet to find and relate to members.

The American Red Cross got some interesting information from a month-long survey on its Web site, though it may not reflect frank answers from a representative sample.

>>> Sixty-nine percent of survey takers were men; 33 percent ages 21-30, 22 percent ages 31-40, 21 percent ages 41-50.

>>> Annual income was under $35,000 for 46 percent and over $75,000 for just 7 percent.

>>> More than one-third volunteer for a Red Cross chapter, 55 percent for other organizations.

>>> Just over half said they were currently contributing to the Red Cross; 57 percent said their annual charitable giving was less than $1,000. (Amazingly, 17 percent said they'd be interested in including the Red Cross in their wills.)

>>> Forty percent of visitors used a 14.4 modem, 31 percent a faster 28.8. The rest had very high-speed connections.

>>> Sixty percent spent at least 15 hours a month on the Internet. How did they get to the Web site? 31 percent from another site, 42 percent from Yahoo or another search engine.

>>> 80 percent said they would approve of the Red Cross accepting corporate sponsors for its Web site "if it supports your efforts and is done professionally."

>>> 58 percent would be interested in getting monthly e-mail news to learn about the Red Cross' "regular and/or large disaster operations."

No free launch

Since most organizations with a Web site or online forum use them mainly for education and activation, it's hard to allocate costs to the few pages within a site devoted to fundraising. The main ongoing Web costs, according to the ACLU's Decker, are salary for the online coordinator; monthly charges for server use, consulting, and services from their technical service provider; credit card processing; and creative and production services for frequent updating of the Web site.

Sending credit card numbers over the Internet is not 100 percent secure yet—but neither is giving it to the waiter.

Many donors are "still skittish," says WPLN's Pope. However, soon Visa, MasterCard, and other vendors will introduce "secure" systems. AT&T is already guaranteeing its new Internet customers against fraud when they use their AT&T-issued Universal Visa and MasterCards for Internet purchases.

As credit card transactions are more accepted and Internet usage skyrockets, getting donations should become easier.

Dealing with the e-mail

If your site is inviting and you invite feedback, you'll get a lot of e-mail requests for information and assistance. Internet users expect quick—if not instant—responses, and good customer relations demands greater speed on the Net than via the mail or fax.

Betsy Jubb of the American Cancer Society says her assistant spends 90 percent of her time answering the more than 100 e-mail queries they receive every day. With little promotion, their site receives over 150,000 hits a month.

Membership services

Wondering how you might use the Internet to build relationships with your members or donors?

Imagine messages like these in their e-mail boxes:

>>> "Thanks to your generous gift, we were able to . . . ."

>>> "Here's what we're doing to help the flood victims in Oregon . . . "

>>> "Click here to fax your member of Congress urging support for H.B. 229. Or write the fax in your own words here and click to send it."

>>> "Visit our Web site to hear the "All Things Considered" story about us from last night . . . "

>>> "Join me for a breakfast briefing next month when I'm in your city . . . "

>>> "Please take 5 minutes to answer these questions about Urgent Issue X and e-mail me your comments."

>>> "Want to participate in our Run Against AIDS next month?"

>>> "Our publications are cataloged at <www.yourorg.org>. Order them online, or download them free."

>>> "Moving? Click here to E-mail us your new address . . . "

>>> "Renew now on-line and get a free BMW!"

Apart from computer-connected organizations like the Electronic Frontier Foundation and Computer Professionals for Social Responsibility, our (limited) research didn't locate any big organizations that systematically use e-mail and the Web for relating to members acquired online, or regular members who might like to communicate electronically (and environmentally).

But we believe the Web is tailor-made for this purpose.

The Electronic Frontier Foundation

One of the 10 most-linked-to sites on the entire World Wide Web.

⚡	Free Speech Online	Private Communications Online	🔑
	Blue Ribbon Campaign	Golden Key Campaign	

The Electronic Frontier Foundation is a non-profit civil liberties organization working in the public interest to protect privacy, free expression, and access to public resources and information in new media.

About EFF	Action ALERTS	Join EFF	Archive Index	Net Guide	Newsletter
Calendar	Board & Staff Homepages	Job Openings	T-shirts, etc.	Awards & Recognition	Other Stuff

Search EFF Archives for: [_____] [Search]

Will find each of 2 or more terms (OR), not just matches containing all terms (AND).

Judges rule 3-0: CDA is unconstitutional!
Enforcement of both "indecency" and "patent offensiveness" statutes is enjoined!
(June 12, 1996).
Full text of decision available.

E-mail messages are far less intrusive than dinner-time phone calls—and they cost virtually nothing. While e-mail comes only in plain-vanilla, one-font format, your e-mails can direct members to your Web site's interactive graphics, sound, video, searchable databases, instant-response quizzes, and more.

If Environmental Donor A loves wildlife, she can "subscribe" to a "listserv" that will automatically send her e-mail updates on wildlife issues. A member who wants to lobby can join your rapid response system, receive automatic alerts, and fax Congress right from the members-only section of your Web site.

The ACLU, for example, offers free subscriptions to four e-mail lists. Their Action Alerts list has over 2,000 subscribers, and their electronic newsletter on cyber-liberty has over 1,500. The Natural Resources Defense Council's "State of Nature" list has thousands of subscribers.

A Web site is open to 30 or 40 million Internet users from Sacramento to Shanghai, but you can also set up password-protected pages as a benefit for "members only." There your members can:

>>> Tell you their views (via surveys or e-mail forms)

>>> Get updates on your work, your successes, upcoming media interviews, and events

>>> Order books, videos, T-shirts or anything else, and pay with a credit card (and member discount!)

>>> Change addresses and perform other housekeeping tasks, or request a call from one of your staff

>>> Renew their membership or make special contributions

>>> Correspond with other members who share their interests or are members of the same chapter.

Taking the next step

First, every time you communicate with your members and donors, ask if they have an e-mail address and if it's OK to communicate with them that way sometimes.

Make sure there's an e-mail field in your database. Put your electronic addresses on all your printed materials. Then start slowly testing what works—and what you can handle—in electronic communication with your members.

If your organization doesn't have a Web site yet, you need to figure out if you need one—how it will advance your mission and goals. Don't put up a Web site just because everyone else is.

If you have a Web site, it makes sense to incorporate fundraising and membership services. Think about how you can use the Web's special dynamic to invite visitors to get involved, learn, and join.

Check out some of the sites listed here to see how the pioneers are experimenting. Consider hiring a consultant who can help. And let me know what's working and what's not.

Check out these sites!

>>> <www.aclu.org> (American Civil Liberties Union)

>>> <www.ran.org> (Rainforest Action Network)

>>> <www.redcross.org> (American Red Cross)

>>> <www.panda.org> (World Wildlife Fund)

>>> <www.wpln.org> (NPR station)

>>> <www.tnc.org> (Nature Conservancy)

>>> <www.cancer.org> (American Cancer Society)

>>> <www.charitiesusa.com/charitiesusa> (Charities U.S.A.)

>>> <www.charityvillage.com/cvhome.html> (Charity Village)

>>> <www.epn.com/auction> (Celebrity Auction)

>>> <www.commerce.com/save_earth> (Artrock Auction)

>>> <www.cooknet.org> (Cookin' on the Net)

>>> <www.impactonline.org> (nonprofit service center)

>>> <www.reliefnet.org>

All World Wide Web addresses start with http://, but you can omit it with Netscape and most other browsers.

Much of this material first appeared in the newsletter Successful Direct Mail & Telephone Fundraising *(July 1996).*

>>>

2

Anatomy of a Web site

by MAL WARWICK

Have you gone Web-surfing lately? Or—just between us—have you been too timid to try? Well, here's your chance to get a whiff of how this Internet stuff really works . . . without all the fuss and bother of getting on the Internet yourself!

That's right: In this chapter, I'll take you with me step by step through one first-rate World Wide Web site. You'll get a peek at the depth, complexity, and variety the Internet offers.

If you're an old hand at roaming the Web, you know perfectly well this is a poor substitute for the actual experience of going online and following your curiosity to its logical (or, more likely, illogical) conclusion. But, unless you've studied this particular Web site, you may learn a thing or two about how one outstanding example of the Webweavers' art has been structured.

So, let's take a look together at what the World Wildlife Fund can tell us through the Internet.

To start the process, I'll open up my CompuServe Mosaic browser and type in the address <www.panda.org>. Voilà! This is what comes up on the screen:

This is a little different from what I'm used to.

Unlike most Web sites I've visited, WWF's doesn't begin with a home page chock full of enticing choices—a page that can take several minutes to load even with my 28,800-baud modem and a fast Pentium computer. In a gesture of civility, WWF instead offers us the choice to "Click here to enter the WWF Global Network." So let's see what happens:

Text Index | Français/Español Check out What's New!

http://www.panda.org/special/quiz5.htm

Here, then, is a more familiar-looking home page. Look at the profusion of choices we're offered: "Sights & Sounds," "Tip of the Day," "Monthly Quiz," and "WWF Survey"—not to mention eight other options, including background on the World Wildlife Fund and its publications and intimate peeks at its programs around the world.

Where to first? Let's check out some of that background material. We'll click on "About WWF" and . . .

ALL ABOUT WWF

- Welcome to WWF!
- What is WWF?
- WWF In Action
- WWF's Priorities
- Help Make A Difference
- Contacting WWF
- Board & Senior Staff
- To the Year 2000 ...
- A History of WWF

Conservation ... it's good for business.

Aha! Another layer of choices! (How many layers of information is that now—three? And we're just getting started!) Let's try "Help Make a Difference":

As part of its Vietnamese Biological Diversity Conservation Study, WWF has developed an action plan to save the country's last 300 to 400 wild elephants.

WWF-South Africa helped save Africa's only penguin species when its last remaining colony was threatened by the Apollo Sea oil spill off the Cape Coast.

In Italy, WWF's Blue and Wild schools are training government representatives and NGO volunteers from all Mediterranean countries in land and marine protected - area management techniques, including "green economics", environmental education, and ecotourism.

Here are color photos (use your imagination!) of three newsworthy World Wildlife Fund projects. The little down arrow on the lower right-hand side of the screen indicates there are more projects where these came from. So let's click on that arrow a few times and scroll down the screen to see what else WWF offers us as ways to help make a difference:

In Sweden, WWF is encouraging school classes to become "nature watchers" by devising conservation programmes that the children can implement themselves.

To teach people how to prevent pollution, WWF - India has, with local organizations, developed low - cost kits for monitoring water and air pollution. WWF now plans to "export" the kits to other countries.

HELP WWF TO MAKE A DIFFERENCE

All those concerned know that WWF's conservation solutions come from practical experience:

- WWF's fieldwork is based on the best scientific information available
- WWF understands the need to involve local communities in every aspect of its work

More cool stuff! And there's *still* more . . .

With another click of the mouse, we come to the end of this particular layer on the Web site. And lo and behold . . .

WWF's work of containing, and eventually reversing, the steady degradation of the world's natural resources demands constant vigilance.

WWF's 4.7 million supporters are vital to this process as they provide the majority of the funds that sustain the organization's work. In addition, their voices add indispensable weight to WWF's message in boardrooms, at international conferences, and in the corridors of power.

⊙ A lasting legacy

"WWF's programme for the next five years is ambitious: to begin to meet the demands of the natural world, WWF must double its public support and its investment in conservation. For this we need your help. "

Ken Phillips
International Development Director

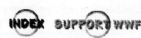

"A lasting legacy!"

To us fundraisers, of course, those are codewords for "bequest." The underlining and the bright color that phrase appears in indicates that clicking on it will take us even more deeply into the Web.site. When we take the hint, here's what we see:

A lasting legacy

"I expect to pass through this life but once. If there be any kindness I can show, let me do it now, as I shall not pass this way again."

William Penn (1644-1718)

The conservation of the natural world is the most precious gift you can leave to your descendants. Through a bequest or assurance policy, you can help protect the earth for future generations.

Bequests

A bequest to WWF can be:

- the residue of your estate after all other provisions have been made
- a percentage of your estate, or a specific amount
- a share portfolio, property, or similar asset.

Assurance policy

By taking out a policy or transferring an existing one to the benefit of WWF, you can

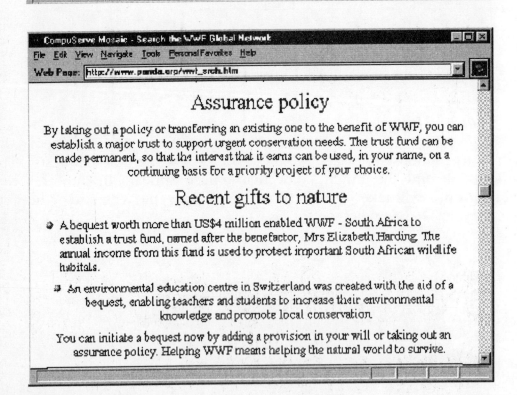

CompuServe Mosaic - Search the WWF Global Network

File Edit View Navigate Tools Personal Favorites Help

Web Page: http://www.panda.org/wwf_srch.htm

Assurance policy

By taking out a policy or transferring an existing one to the benefit of WWF, you can establish a major trust to support urgent conservation needs. The trust fund can be made permanent, so that the interest that it earns can be used, in your name, on a continuing basis for a priority project of your choice.

Recent gifts to nature

- A bequest worth more than US$4 million enabled WWF - South Africa to establish a trust fund, named after the benefactor, Mrs Elizabeth Harding. The annual income from this fund is used to protect important South African wildlife habitats.

- An environmental education centre in Switzerland was created with the aid of a bequest, enabling teachers and students to increase their environmental knowledge and promote local conservation.

You can initiate a bequest now by adding a provision in your will or taking out an assurance policy. Helping WWF means helping the natural world to survive.

Now let's backtrack to the WWF home page and try another path through the labyrinth of information at this site. We'll click on "Ways to Contact WWF," and this is what happens:

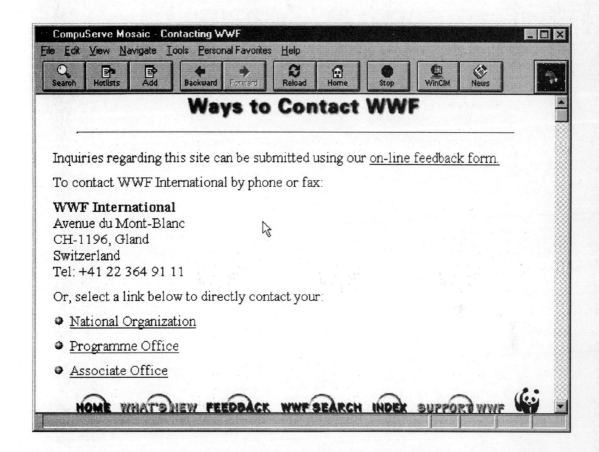

There's one of those scroll-bars again! So there's lots more to see on this page. And remember: Each of those underlined, brightly-colored phrases will take us on a new path through the labyrinth. But instead let's zip back to the home page and check out another option: "What's New." Here it comes . . .

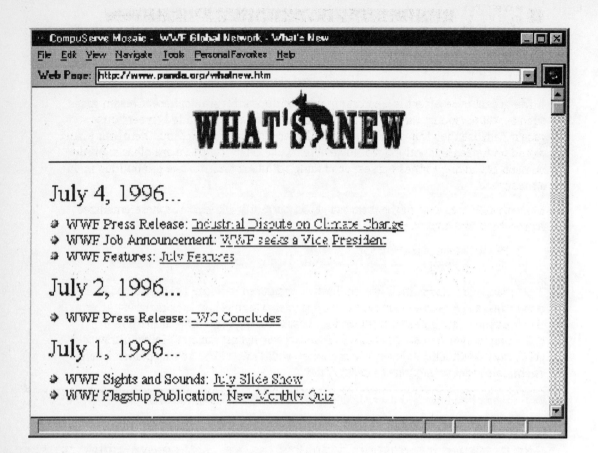

Hmmm! These folks are really on the ball. Just look at how frequently they update their Web site with new information! But I'm a little bored with all this scrolling. I'm ready to *do* something online. So I'd like you to join me in checking out the "New Monthly Quiz" (the second entry under "July 1, 1996").

Here goes:

This month's quiz: *Climate*

1. The greenhouse effect is a natural feature of the earth's atmosphere. Certain gases, such as water vapour, carbon dioxide, CO2, and methane, are called "greenhouse gases" because they trap solar heat in the lower atmosphere. Without them, our planet would be frozen and nothing would be able to live on it. But there are clear signs that humans are adding to these gases, producing pollutants that cause a gas buildup in the atmosphere.

More than 90 per cent of the manmade CO2 currently in the atmosphere emanated from which two countries?

- ☐ North America and Europe
- ☐ Japan and Africa

2. Human, plant, and animal life on Earth is protected by a fragile shroud or layer of ozone gas, a naturally occurring form of oxygen which is highly poisonous. At ground level, ozone contributes to smog and acid rain. But high up in the stratosphere (25-30km above the earth), ozone forms a screen against the sun's lethal ultraviolet (UV) rays. Without this layer, UV radiation would kill all life on this planet. Many chemicals react with ozone to destroy it.

Pretty dense information, wouldn't you say? Let's move a little further down:

What is the most destructive chemical to the ozone?

- ☐ Nitric and nitrous oxides from vehicle exhausts
- ☐ Chloro-fluorocarbons (CFCs)
- ☐ Carbon dioxide produced by burning fossil fuels
- ☐ Halons and methyl bromide (used as a pesticide)

3. According to historical temperature records, what decade was the warmest on record?

- ☐ 1960s
- ☐ 1970s
- ☐ 1980s
- ☐ 1990s

4. As the world swelters and global weather patterns seem on the verge of spiraling out of control, scientists believe the climate is changing faster than at any time in the last 10,000 years. The situation is so serious, and the threat to many of the wo rld's most precious species and ecosystems so grave, that WWF has launched a major new campaign to try and halt climate change.

One of the goals is to reduce CO_2 emissions by at least what percent?

- ☐ 5%
- ☐ 15%
- ☐ 50%
- ☐ 20%

And, while we're at it, let's go on to the end of the quiz . . .

5. The greenhouse effect is no myth. It is a natural feature of the atmosphere. Certain gases, such as water vapour, carbon dioxide (CO_2), and meth-ane, are called greenhouse gases because they trap solar heat in the lower atmosphere. Of the three gases listed, what is the most important?

- ◯ Water Vapour
- ◯ Carbon Dioxide
- ◯ Meth-ane

Please complete the following section before pressing the submit button:

Name:	Ms. ▼ First: [ ]	Last: [ ]
Address:	[ ]	
Address:	[ ]	
City:	[ ]	
State:	select ▼	
Country:	[ ]	
Post Code:	[ ]	
Phone:	[ ]	
E-Mail:	[ ]	

The plot thickens!

By completing this quiz—including the personal information requested in the form shown above—I can be sure to find my way onto the World Wildlife Fund database (if I'm not already there). And if I'm currently a member, WWF will have that much more information on file about me.

For one thing, they'll know I respond to involvement opportunities like this. And that's invaluable knowledge, as any fundraiser can easily imagine.

But the monthly quiz is only one such involvement device on this marvelous site. Let's slip backwards to the home page again and check out the "WWF Survey":

■ WWF SURVEY

1. After visiting the WWF site, in general, you have found it to be...

1. ◉ One of the very best sites on the Internet.
2. ☐ An above average site.
3. ☐ An average site.
4. ☐ A poor site.
5. ☐ No opinion.

Comments:

2. Specifically, you found the *content* of the site to be...

1. ◉ Excellent.
2. ☐ Above average.
3. ☐ Average.
4. ☐ Poor.
5. ☐ Don't Know, Skip.

Comments:

3. Specifically, you found the *graphical presentation* of the site to be...

Is this a *truly* impartial survey? Probably not. The top ratings are already checked here. To register different choices, I'll need to check other boxes. But, hey—I don't resent the hint! And the effort to move the mouse is, after all, not onerous.

So let's look further:

3. Specifically, you found the *graphical presentation* of the site to be...

1. ◉ Excellent.
2. ○ Average.
3. ○ Poor.
4. ○ Don't Know, Skip.

Comments:

[ ]

4. After exploring the WWF site, you will visit...

1. ◉ Daily.
2. ○ Weekly.
3. ○ Monthly.
4. ○ Rarely.
5. ○ Never.
6. ○ Don't Know, Skip.

Comments:

[ ]

5. You would consider the progress of the conservation movement to be ...

And so on:

5. You would consider the progress of the conservation movement to be ...

1. ☐ Excellent.
2. ☐ Good.
3. ☐ Only Fair.
4. ☐ Poor.
5. ◉ Don't Know, Skip.

Comments:

6. Did you find this site was logically organized, allowing for ease of use?

Comments:

7. What features of this site did you find most/least interesting?

Comments:

And on to the end:

Thank you for taking part in this very important survey. Please also include your personal information below.

First Name:

Last Name:

E-mail Address:

Mailing Address:

City:

State:

Country:

Postal Code:

Voice Phone:

Fax:

Comments:

So here's one more golden opportunity for the World Wildlife Fund to learn about me—and for me to become more involved in the Fund!

And let's not lose sight of how much time, effort, and thought goes into maintaining this Web site. Here, for example, is the "Tip of the Day." (Got that? The tip of the *day*! These folks update the information posted on their site almost every day of the year!)

Remember: bicycles, public transport, and your own two feet are far kinder to the environment.

WWF aims to conserve nature and ecological processes by:

◆ preserving genetic, species, and ecosystem diversity
◆ ensuring that the use of renewable natural resources is sustainable both now and in the longer term
◆ promoting actions to reduce pollution and the wasteful exploitation and consumption of energy

<u>Another Tip Please!!!</u>

   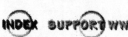

Copyright 1996, The World Wide Fund For Nature

Cool, isn't it?

Cool enough to move you to join the World Wildlife Fund? Here's what happens when you get the urge to do so online:

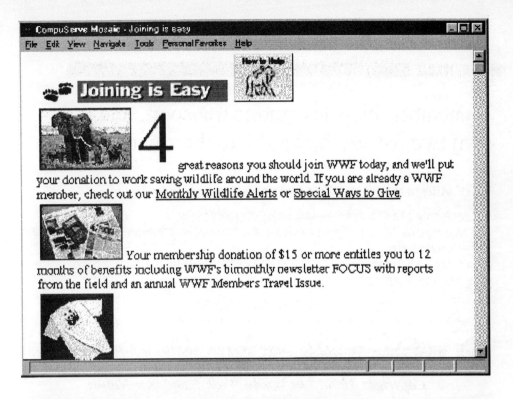

Joining is Easy

4 great reasons you should join WWF today, and we'll put your donation to work saving wildlife around the world. If you are already a WWF member, check out our Monthly Wildlife Alerts or Special Ways to Give.

Your membership donation of $15 or more entitles you to 12 months of benefits including WWF's bimonthly newsletter FOCUS with reports from the field and an annual WWF Members Travel Issue.

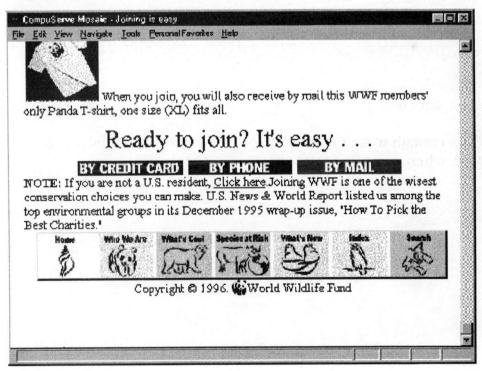

When you join, you will also receive by mail this WWF members' only Panda T-shirt, one size (XL) fits all.

Ready to join? It's easy . . .

BY CREDIT CARD　**BY PHONE**　**BY MAIL**

NOTE: If you are not a U.S. resident, Click here. Joining WWF is one of the wisest conservation choices you can make. U.S. News & World Report listed us among the top environmental groups in its December 1995 wrap-up issue, 'How To Pick the Best Charities.'

Copyright © 1996. World Wildlife Fund

3

Tools you can use online

by MICHAEL STEIN

O kay, now let's get past all the techno-jargon. Here are some of the basic tools you can use to make your Internet efforts successful—demystified, and explained in plain English.

E-mail

E-mail is the most used Internet tool, far surpassing the World Wide Web. Many people who don't have access to the Web have e-mail at their desks. In more and more offices, people can exchange e-mail with anyone on the Internet.

For an organization, it's important to develop good e-mail habits. First of all, set up one main e-mail contact account, and publicize it frequently and prominently.

For example—to pick a hypothetical organization—the "Campaign for Justice" should establish an address such as "<cfj@cfj.org>". (Contact your Internet Service Provider to set up such an account.)

It's better not to use "personal" accounts for this type of communication. If Maria Lopez works at the Campaign for Justice, using an e-mail account called "<mlopez@cfj.org>" is OK. But then you set an expectation that Maria will be the person responding.

Since one of your goals is to use volunteers and interns to help screen incoming e-mail, the use of a "generic" account is therefore more practical. Of course, having e-mail contact with a member of the staff is important, but not for general inquiries. Consider your main e-mail contact account as your first "filter," where most inquiries can be screened, before a regular member of staff needs to become involved.

Many organizations have staff members who are highly visible campaigners. Having these staff people devote two or three hours each week to replying to e-mail can pay off by impressing your members or prospective members with the openness and availability of staff to membership interaction. But be sure to define the boundaries of this correspondence, or three hours can easily grow to eight.

Make your main e-mail address visible on business cards, brochures, newsletters, flyers, press releases, and on any online media such as mailing lists or Web sites. This address will get onto resource lists that are published and may be in print for several years, so be sure to not change it. If you have to, be sure to set up forwarding tools (similar to mail and phone forwarding) to assure smooth continuity.

Nothing discourages your correspondents more than having e-mail returned as "undeliverable."

Monitor your main e-mail account at least once a day, and reply promptly to messages. The key is to constantly maintain the appearance that you're committed to keeping e-mail contact. If you reply infrequently to messages received, then you'll disappoint your correspondents and create the impression you're not serious about using the medium.

You will quickly notice a pattern to the types of questions and issues raised in e-mail. Consider having a set of "standard" replies ready. One useful tool is a "Frequently Asked Questions" (FAQ) file that, if updated regularly, can be a quick way to reply to messages.

Many messages won't fall into a pattern. They'll require composed and thoughtful e-mail response. Don't treat this type of personal communication lightly. Many of your e-mail correspondents will be naturally skeptical about the benefits of the on-line medium, and will respond very positively to alert and personal responses. This is particularly important if your organization is starting out with a new online campaign. Avoid disappointing people early on—you'll set a bad example.

If you find yourself communicating with current members—don't hesitate to determine this early on!—you'll discover that maintaining e-mail contact is a good way to keep a communication channel open with a minimum of time commitment.

Infobots and auto-replies

An "infobot" or "auto-reply" is a form of automatic e-mail with its own Internet e-mail address. You set up an auto-reply with an Internet Service Provider, and promote it along with your main e-mail contact account.

When someone sends e-mail to the auto-reply, it will automatically send back an electronic document containing information pertinent to your work—with no human intervention required. Your Internet Service Provider will help you choose good names for your auto-replies.

The fictitious Campaign for Justice might set up "<cfj-info@cfj.org>" or "<cfj-immigration@cfj.org>" to distribute automatic electronic updates on the organization in general or about the Campaign for Justice's "Immigrant Rights Campaign."

Don't forget to keep the information in the auto-reply current, accurate, and useful. Try to anticipate the questions people will have—to minimize the need for further contact. If you advertise a new campaign video but forget to tell people how to order it, then you can expect dozens of e-mail messages inquiring how to obtain copies. You can spare a lot of effort by including more complete information.

You should expect to receive a weekly or monthly log of the number of "hits" your auto-reply has received. Auto-reply "hit logs" are very informative. They should show you the complete e-mail address of the person who requested the information, which is far more useful than the information obtained from your World Wide Web hit logs. This list of e-mail addresses can become a way to market your organization's agenda.

You might try sending a short e-mail to the list each month saying something like: "You recently requested information about the Campaign for Justice by e-mail. We encourage your participation in our other online activities such as our Internet mailing list, or public Web site. We also encourage you to become a member of the Campaign for Justice to support our important work in this area, and this will give you access to our members-only Web site and private discussion group." This is a form of prospecting, since many people who use auto-replies will be prospective members who are getting basic information about your work.

An auto-reply is an effective way to distribute information that's unwieldy to distribute through other means. When the Environmental Defense Fund released a 1994 report on the danger of lead in china plates, the organization widely advertised an auto-reply address to distribute the complete and exhaustive list of brands implicated. The list was simply too long to distribute as part of the press release. This auto-reply address got several thousand hits in a few months.

Listservs and mailing lists

"Listservs" and "mailing lists" are Internet discussion groups where people congregate to discuss issues and exchange information. A mailing list is a "group" of e-mail accounts that are tied together through a central e-mail address. Each mailing list has a theme or subject and people will "join" this mailing list and expect to participate in discussion or information exchange about that subject.

We suggest that organizations set up a "main" Internet discussion group devoted to a major campaign or project that the organization is working on. That way, members or supporters who want to stay up-to-date on campaign activities, or are keen to meet other activists, can interact with one another in a focused way.

Listservs can also be a useful way to offer multiple discussion forums for several different issues. But if you have only one mailing list for all your campaigns, your subscribers may be confused about which issue is being discussed. People are often single-issue oriented. So's it's usually easier to have multiple mailing lists for separate issues.

If a mailing list gets little or no activity, close it. A "stale" mailing list disappoints people and is a poor reflection on your organization's agenda, much like a meeting or event few people attend.

Contact your Internet Service Provider to discuss options and prices for setting up and running mailing lists.

At the outset, you'll have to decide whether to make the subscription process "open" or "closed."

>>> If a mailing list subscription is "open," anyone can join the mailing list, regardless of whether they're members or supporters. It can be very beneficial to have open lists, because they require less work and are good marketing and communication tools. However, open lists can attract "unwanted" people, including opponents of your campaigns who want to stir up confrontational debate or engage in discussions that may detract from your goals.

>>> "Closed" mailing lists allow you to screen people who want to join. You'll have to approve or disapprove each subscription request manually. This can be time-consuming. But it affords a certain amount of quality control. If you're very concerned about screening your participants, you might require phone contact to verify a person's identity. This practice is rare but not unknown.

Another important question is whether to maintain a "moderated" list. With a moderated list, you have the ability to screen people's comments and contributions to the mailing list. This is extremely time-consuming if you intend the mailing list to be discussion-based, and certainly not practical. Organizations usually set up "moderation" because they intend the mailing list to be a "one-way" feed of information to the subscribers.

For example, the Pesticide Action Network has a weekly news service called PANUPS (the Pesticide Action Network Updates Service) which is distributed in this way. They have an "open" mailing list which is "moderated." Several hundred subscribers receive the weekly PANUPS news bulletins. The mailing list is not advertised as being a discussion list, so people rarely write to the mailing list with questions or comments. If they do, the messages are automatically "diverted" to the Pesticide Action Network's main e-mail contact account.

To promote membership and fundraising development, you might consider allowing people to subscribe to a "private" (or "closed") mailing list as a membership benefit. Similar in kind to mailing a membership print newsletter, an electronic news bulletin distributed in this way will be a way to reinforce the benefits of membership in your organization.

Be sure the content of this electronic newsletter is different from your print newsletter! Otherwise, people will have already seen the content. This is a good way to distribute urgent actions. The "urgency" of e-mail will reinforce this. Such a Rapid Response Network can be a key way to mobilize your members to join you in campaigns and projects.

World Wide Web sites

Web sites are so talked about today that you should consider them an essential online tool. For membership development and fundraising, they're vital. Developed and maintained regularly, a Web site provides an easy way to interact with your membership, to reinforce their contributions, and ask for more. Web sites are less intrusive than phone calls, and certainly more enjoyable than direct mail.

Web sites are important Internet tools. But they shouldn't be used exclusively to the neglect of e-mail, auto-replies, or mailing lists. Remember that many of your members won't have explored the Web yet—but they may be e-mail pros.

A Web site can be an important and effective way to get out the message of your organization, and to reinforce how important membership is. A Web site will attract both current and prospective members. By advertising your Web site address through your mailings, brochures, fundraising appeals, and newsletters, you can assure a steady flow of members who are curious about what your Web site has to offer.

Be sure your Web site isn't just a repackaging of your regular materials. That way your current members will quickly lose interest. However, many prospective members will be browsing your material for the first time, so don't neglect your basic material.

One strategy for dealing with this challenge is to offer a public and free Web site for anyone to browse. Then consider offering a members-only section of the Web site where people who are already members can get "more" and "special" information. This becomes a good location to place further appeals for support. Don't be too forceful in the appeal, but don't neglect it. This members-only section is a good place to put personal messages from a Board Member or the campaign director.

Consider ways to make this message current and personal by changing the message frequently. The message can be written, or you can use audio messages using technologies such as RealAudio (see below).

One key to a good Web site is to make it entertaining and interesting. Try to highlight what is "new" and "updated." Feature "alerts."

Graphics are important, but make them very small (so they "load" quickly even with a slower modem). People will appreciate it and return to your site.

Several new Web technologies can make your Web site more entertaining, and you might consider using some of them to "animate" your site.

>>> A "server push" allows you to make images move as sequential frames. A good example of this is the moving jaguar on the Rainforest Action Network Web site (http://www.ran.org).

>>> Other technologies include Shockwave and Java animations, which can animate images and graphics for even more effect.

While the results can be impressive, the number of your viewers who can experience these multimedia tools is somewhat limited at this time, though numbers are growing. For those using relatively "slow" modems (2,400 to 14,400 baud), these technologies work imperfectly if at all. Also, consider the public relations implications of having a Web site that's so "advanced" many of your members can't view it fully! We consider it advisable not to let the more technologically adept members completely dominate the technology of your Web site. But keep in mind their enthusiasm—it's a key asset in developing and maintaining your site.

You don't have to use these innovative devices to build and maintain a good Web site. In fact, the bells and whistles described above can backfire if you don't have good content in your Web site.

Think about assembling the material of your Web site in the same way you publish a newsletter, brochure, or annual report. Don't get too text-heavy to begin with—but be sure to make longer text materials available for those viewers who come seeking your complete reports, background documents, and so on.

Make sure you're offering ways for people to send you e-mail from your Web site. Promote your main e-mail contact address so your members—and prospective members—can contact you directly.

Web sites can be effective by offering basic and easy-to-use tools such as search buttons. If members and others will come to your Web site looking for information about Mexico (for example), implement a search tool that makes this easy to find—or otherwise many of your visitors may get lost in your site looking for the information.

You might *think* you're building an easy-to-use and smoothly navigable Web site. But odds are you'll lose people who won't understand your site structure. Take feedback seriously, since it'll help you maintain a better site and show that you're open to criticism and participation.

More and more discussion areas are appearing on Web sites. Similar in function to Internet mailing lists, they exist only within the Web site. Discussion areas or "forums" require that people come back to the site again and again. This can be a challenge, as it competes for attention span with e-mail. Web discussion areas can be technical challenges to maintain. But the technology seems to be improving, which will no doubt increase their use.

Money transfers on the Internet are still the exception rather than the rule. If you're seeking contributions or new members online, it's best to offer a choice of methods for sending the money: a phone number, a toll-free number, or the mail as well as online credit card transactions.

While some people are reluctant to give their credit card number over the Internet, or to use one of the electronic cash mechanisms (CyberCash, First Virtual Bank, etc.), these direct Web transactions are gaining in trust and popularity. As major financial institutions such as Visa, American Express, and others join in this practice, the popularity of these tools will increase.

Online services

Online services such as America Online and CompuServe maintain huge members-only subscription networks. While members of these networks have access to the Web and can get to your Web site, you might consider also having a presence on these networks to reach out more effectively.

For instance, the Campaign for Justice might consider joining the "Immigration Forum" on CompuServe to let people know about its current campaign, and advertise its auto-reply, e-mail, and Web site addresses.

Doing bold membership appeals on those networks can often backfire, so set your goal to attract members to your other online tools. Let them do the fundraising work for you. Having a presence on other networks can be an excellent focused project for an intern or volunteer who has these skills.

It's important to integrate the online medium with your other membership development efforts, and not to relegate it to the sideline. In developing online content, you can start with much of the material and graphic elements you've already developed for the print, video, and audio media—and then take off from there.

Remember, the key is finding new and exciting ways to interact with your membership, to make them excited about being a part of your campaigns, and to reward their participation and financial contribution. So make sure interaction, excitement, and reward are at the heart of your online efforts.

How to get people to your site . . . again and again

Publicizing your e-mail and URL

You have to be *serious* about publishing your online addresses—your main e-mail contact and your Web site—in as many places as possible. Put those addresses on your business cards, your brochures, your newsletters, your printed reports, your stationery, and any press release you put out. Only by taking advantage of every publicity opportunity open to you will you be able to convey the message to your membership that you've begun to use the online medium in earnest.

Keep in mind that informing people of your online addresses means you have to be diligent about replying to your e-mail and keeping your Web site up-to-date. Thoroughness requires consistent follow-through and delivery!

Another important way to publicize your e-mail and URL addresses is to make sure everyone involved with your organization is competent to use the basic online tools. By this we mean your staff, your volunteers and interns, your board members, and so on. This basic internal education campaign will make people feel a part of your effort, and will allow everyone to be a part of the publicity effort. You'll also challenge patterns of technological literacy whereby some people know this stuff and others don't.

Another key aspect to publicizing your e-mail and URL is to inform people in your issue area and constituency that you now have these addresses available. Consider a one-page fact sheet you can include in your next mailing to allies and friends.

Don't go to your next coalition meeting or conference without your fact sheets so you really tap the strength of your movement. You want to build a "buzz" that you have these new online tools. On the Internet, "buzz" is a key to success.

Getting and keeping links

The real key to success is hard work. Publicizing your online presence is going to require many hours to surf the Net and place announcements about your Web site in other sites. These Web announcements are often referred to as "links."

Consider visiting the many electronic white and yellow pages that have cropped up. All these sites—such as Yahoo!, Netscape, InfoSeek, etc.—have submission forms for you to list your new site. You'll have to do much of this work manually, methodically, and repeatedly.

This is a good place to involve interns and volunteers since it's very practical and defined. Be sure to visit these sites a week later to make sure your site has been properly listed.

Another form of publicity is to visit other Web sites that cover issues similar to your own and to "exchange" links. This is a valuable form of publicity, since people go to one site to look for material, and then naturally want to look at related material.

Of course, your own site will have to have links to other sites. In regard to working with allies to exchange links, don't hesitate to pick up the phone to set this up. It often works more effectively than e-mail, and you'll establish direct contact with other Webweavers.

Measuring success

There are three key ways to measure your success on the Internet.

>>> The first is to assess whether you're actually building traffic and audience for your e-mail, auto-reply, mailing list, and Web site. You should be able to assess this by keeping regular tabs on the numbers of your incoming e-mails, hits to your auto-replies, subscribers to your mailing lists, and hits to your Web site. Don't worry too much about the sheer number or about comparing yourself to others. Your concern is steady growth in the amount of activity as your members begin to use this medium. Traffic should build steadily and should peak as you do special promotions or marketing.

>>> The second way to measure success is in the feedback you get from your members. They may be your best measure, since you're doing this all for them. Ask them at meetings, ask them over the phone, ask them by e-mail, do online surveys—do anything you can to solicit their involvement in using the medium. Ask them flat out: "What would it take for you to take this medium and our involvement seriously?"

>>> The third way to measure success is whether you're raising money from this effort. Don't forget to ask people why they gave you money. If you have membership forms with check boxes, add one for "Internet/Web," or you'll never know why and how they gave. In your donor database, set up a code to track online activity and interest. Of course, if you're actually collecting money over the Net, using such tools as First Virtual, CyberCash, or secure commerce, it will be easy to track. But make sure you add information about each transaction to your database, or this valuable data will be lost.

Staff time and resources to keep your site current

One critical aspect to the success of your online fundraising efforts is the amount of staff time and resources you devote. The costs in equipment and Internet services are likely to be easily definable and containable. Staff time is scalable: The more staff time you can devote to this effort, the more successful your results.

You'll need at least a quarter-time staff person to manage your online efforts. A half-timer is better. Replying to e-mail, maintaining your Web site, keeping links up-to-date, working with your membership department to coordinate activities, developing new multimedia for your site, coordinating interns and volunteers that will do some of the work for you—all these activities take time. If you're not prepared to devote some staff time to this activity, then don't do it. If you go into this half-heartedly, you'll waste your money and disappoint members who expect quick responses and new Web content on a regular basis.

>>>

4

Fundraising opportunities online

by MICHAEL JOHNSTON

As a charitable fundraiser you do not want to be left behind by other practitioners when a new fundraising medium comes onto the scene.

Yet the pressure of being forced to master a new fundraising medium, when you are still working on the "ins" and "outs" of direct mail, telephone, and television fundraising, is more stress you just do not need.

Now, with the frenzied press coverage of the Internet, you are being asked (or are about to be!) by staff, volunteers, and board members about the fundraising potential of this new electronic medium.

This article will show you that there are as many fundraising opportunities online as there are in the "real" vs. "virtual" world. Fundraisers have never been stumped for new fundraising ideas—and it will be no different online.

There are three questions that you, as a nonprofit manager, staff person, or volunteer, should be asking about the Internet:

>>>   Should we get online?

>>>   What are other groups up to with the Internet?

>>>   Will it be profitable to our organization to use the Internet for fund-raising purposes?

The answers are yes, a lot, and with time.

There is no doubt your organization has to get online. There are already too many people on the Internet now to ignore—and in the future there will be a great many more.

It is a new medium that nonprofit organizations are already using to reach a wider audience to help them accomplish their mission and mandate —including new ways to raise money. Every charity should make the small investment needed to make it a part of its media mix.

Nicholas Negroponte, a recognized authority on the Internet, estimates that 50 million people are accessing it on a regular basis and there are 100,000 new Internet e-mail addresses being added each month.

Many charities are now using computers for desktop publishing and database management. They already have the physical resources to use the Internet for fundraising and the opportunity to build a new, younger, wealthier constituency. It should not cost more than a few hundred dollars to get on the Internet—perhaps up to a few thousand dollars, but no more.

The World Wide Web (WWW)

The World Wide Web is the fastest growing part of the Internet. On the Web, "pages" of hypertext can be browsed, almost like flipping through the pages of a magazine—complete with pictures, graphics, and even sound and video clips. Individuals and organizations can publish their own "Home Pages" by storing them on a computer that is connected to the Internet and letting interested individuals come and browse the site.

The World Wide Web, because of its capabilities and ease of use, appears destined to become the future of the Internet—for a while anyway. The WWW is a place where organizations are publishing for a wider audience and for their own niche constituencies.

The majority of new Internet users are coming online and are using the World Wide Web to find information, browse, research, chat, and now, make donations to their charities.

Since other fundraising channels are becoming more competitive and cluttered with solicitations, your colleagues are looking to gain the competitive edge.

Now it's time to explain what is being accomplished on the Internet so you can begin to choose how you will participate.

Internet users can be a valuable resource to all charities.

According to a FIND/SVP Survey published in the June 1995 edition of the U.S. magazine *Internet World*, the average household income of a wired family was $66,700 compared to $42,400. I am sure the same is true of Internet users in the U.K. or Canada.

Internet users are utilizing their computers to change their lives with 41% of them telecommuting to work versus 19% of the entire workforce. Internet people work online, even to fulfill more of their consumer needs. Part of their fulfilment can be of a philanthropic nature.

Furthermore:

>>> 81% of Internet users are university graduates versus 33% of all of society.

>>> 40% already own a CD ROM versus 6% of the rest of society.

>>> 12% bank by modem—versus 1% of society as a whole—meaning they are doing things financially online.

>>> 24% are purchasing things online versus 2% of the rest of society.

This group of current Internet users are already sophisticated users of online services and technology. They may turn part of their attention to online philanthropy, if charities learn to use this new medium in a way that gets their attention and pocketbooks.

Moreover, other studies have shown that there is a disproportionate number of younger people who are on the Internet. This is a demographic slice of the pie that charities have been struggling to reach—unsuccessfully in many cases—with more traditional fundraising channels like direct mail. With the incredible growth of the Internet, there are more people coming online who will change the current demographic image of a younger, highly educated, upper income white male to one with a better gender balance and more ethnic and socio-economic diversity.

Now, just what are charities around the world doing on the Internet to raise money?

The Sierra Club: the membership form

This North American-based charity has created an Internet site on the World Wide Web that explains who they are, gives up-to-date campaign information, and provides a membership donation area for Internet visitors. (See **<http://www.sierraclub.org/signature/>**.)

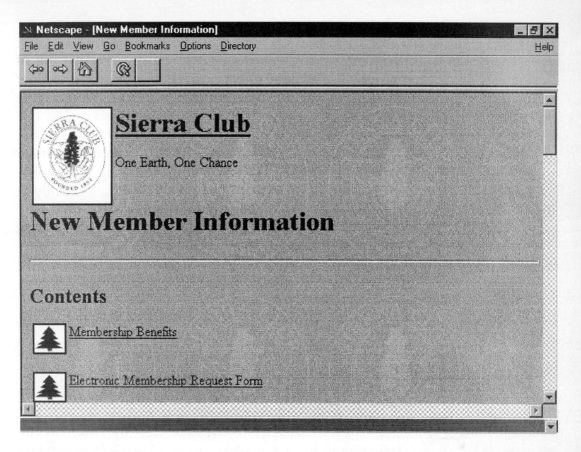

Visitors can print off an order form on their printer and send it back by fax, or they can print it off and send it by snail mail (regular pony express-ground delivery), or they can call a phone number to become a member.

Finally, visitors can fill out an electronic form which sends their name and address to the Sierra Club by e-mail and the Sierra Club can fulfill their membership pledge by regular mail.

Over the last 6 ½ months, since the membership form has been on the Internet, 320 people have made a pledge to join as members. The final numbers have not been tabulated.

However, the Sierra Club has no direct electronic form that allows for instantaneous credit card donation.

Future fundraising possibilities for membership services

Many charities are able to offer expert opinion through a variety of sources.

Now that information can be available online.

Kevin Hall of the National Heart Support Association - Heartwise, says, "we are hoping to get an Internet connection in enabling us to run a 24-hour real-time counseling service via IRC (Inter Relay Chat) which means people will be able to communicate by typing on line with a live expert on heart matters."

Many organizations charge a membership fee to pay for the cost incurred by the charity to provide members with benefits—like access to expert opinion.

The ongoing cost of maintaining a membership area could be met, in part, by a supplemental payment above a regular membership fee—or it could be an extra benefit and incentive without an extra fee.

One way to guarantee the value of an Internet membership would be the creation of an area only accessible with a password—given solely to paying members.

Other areas which give more public information could be free for all visitors—allowing agencies to meet their mandate while generating much needed revenue.

There are a number of charities in Canada which are looking at providing fees for access to certain Internet areas.

Security issues around the Internet

If you are already giving your credit card over the phone to make a charitable donation or order other products (not common in the U.K.) or are filling out a written form using your credit card information and mailing it, then you are already exposed to the dangers of fraud.

Credit card donations over the Internet are as safe (or unsafe) as giving your credit card number over a cellular phone.

There are many Internet users who are making commercial online purchases on secure and unsecured Internet sites. Many nonprofit organizations have decided to provide a range of giving options on their sites.

The Rainforest Action Network: online donation form

This extensive site has everything from action up-dates to a Kid's Korner (**<http://www.ran.org>**). And in the area of fundraising, like the Sierra Club, it has a membership and donation form where people can donate by phone, fax, or mail.

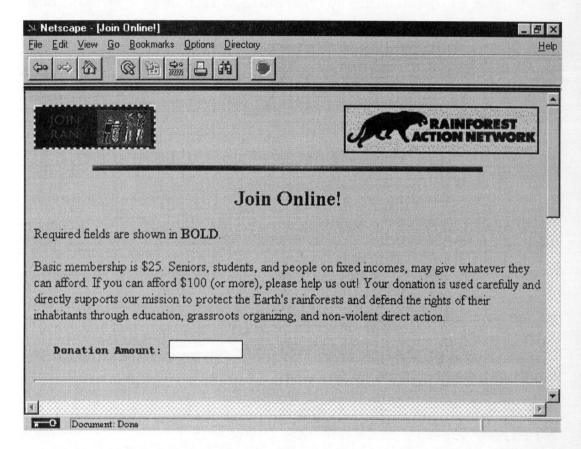

However, they have added an online credit card form, where individuals can zoom their credit card directly to the Rainforest Action Network. They have received donations directly by this method, but they don't have exact numbers.

The Body Shop: selling products

The Body Shop Canada's STOP Violence Against Women Internet site was created by Hewitt and Johnston Consultants, in conjunction with the YWCA of Canada and the Canadian Women's Foundation. (See **<http://www.the-body-shop.ca/power>**.)

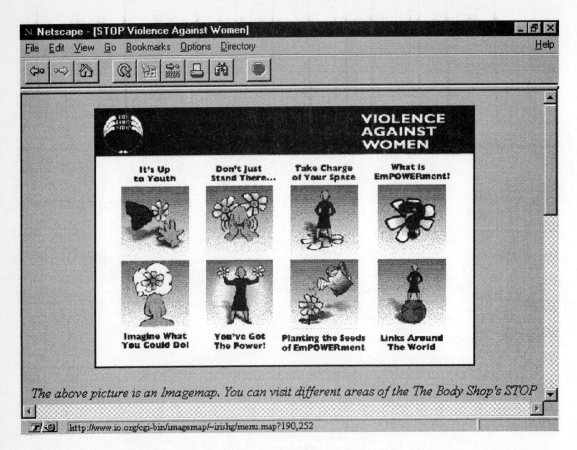

VIOLENCE AGAINST WOMEN

It's Up to Youth

Don't Just Stand There...

Take Charge of Your Space

What is EmPOWERment?

Imagine What You Could Do!

You've Got The Power!

Planting the Seeds of EmPOWERment

Links Around The World

The above picture is an Imagemap. You can visit different areas of the The Body Shop's STOP

http://www.io.org/cgi-bin/imagemap/~irishg/menu.map?190,252

This site was designed to educate and motivate individuals, organizations, schools, and journalists to take action around the issues of violence against women.

To help raise money for the cross-Canada campaign, an online order form makes it possible for interested visitors to order a series of fundraising products: T-Shirts, flower packets, and educational broadsheets.

The credit card orders were sent to an e-mail box monitored by The Body Shop, who fulfilled the orders for the charitable partners.

Since April 1995, orders have come in from as far away as Australia and across Canada. The orders have amounted to only a few hundred dollars, but it is an online campaign that expects to stay on the Internet for years to come, and it's expected that online sales will continue through the online campaign.

There have been no online security problems.

The National Heart Support Association - Heartwise, a United Kingdom health charity, has created a new web site that welcomes visitors by telling them about their chance to win a cash prize if they register with Heartwise. (See **‹http://www.ibmpcug.co.uk/~rwall›.**)

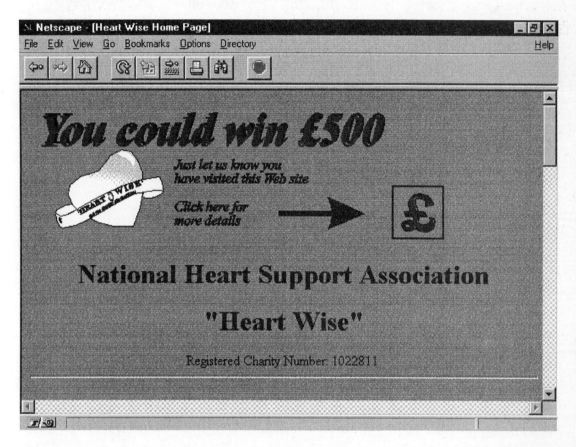

After only one month online, one third of the 530 visitors to their site have entered the lottery. This is an excellent chance to get the names, address, and e-mail address of these individuals to begin an e-mail relationship with this electronic stakeholder group.

The opportunities for raising money with online games of chance are endless, but it is important to make sure you are not breaking laws that regulate charitable games of chance in your state or country.

Easter Seal Society of Ontario: corporate sponsorship

Many nonprofit organizations are finding their corporate supporters—who have traditionally given them financial, product, and volunteer support—are very receptive to sponsoring the creation and upkeep of a Web site for a charity, if they are given the proper recognition for that sponsorship.

In addition, there is an opportunity to link your site to that corporate sponsor for their financial support in the ongoing costs of keeping your site vital and up-to-date.

The Easter Seal Society of Ontario, a Canadian charity that helps disabled children, found a corporate sponsor, MediTrust Pharmacy, who paid for the construction and upkeep of the site. The pharmacy has a link to its own corporate web site (**<http://www.cyberplex.com/CyberPlex/Easter Seals.html>**).

It's one thing to get corporate support to create your Web site, but what do you do once it's up and running to raise more corporate dollars?

Can you charge for advertising—and what do you charge corporations to advertise on your site?

Well, there are some formulas for working out an advertising rate by calculating the number of visits (hits) to the Internet page that a corporation wants to advertise on.

Separate from calculating the advertising value of your site, there is the intangible value of your organization putting its good name in association with a corporate sponsor. That alone is worth a good deal of money.

Finally, if a nonprofit organization has a newsletter or magazine, there is an opportunity to put your publications online, and if you have regular advertisers, they can be charged an Internet supplement to be put on your Web site in the publication area.

There are a number of commercial magazines in the U.S., Canada, and the U.K. that are already publishing their magazines on the Internet and have begun to create a body of experience on charging their regular advertisers on the Internet. Talk to them.

The Canadian Diabetes Association is preparing to publish its national magazine, *Dialogue*, on the Internet and it is preparing to contact current advertisers and ask them to pay a supplement in order to be included on the online version of the magazine.

Some Web sites get thousands of visitors a week, and some get hundreds. If a web site is designed to be fun, informative, and a definitive place to be, then nonprofits can attract a large number of visitors.

NetBenefit and America Online: joining a club

The examples up to this point are Internet endeavors undertaken by each organization, alone. They link to other organizations by their own choice—but their address is theirs alone.

However, a number of Internet sites are communal places that are trying to bring the benefits of collectivity to Internet fundraising.

NetBenefit is a nonprofit corporation that has decided to offer the Internet community an alternative to traditional buying. Consumers can buy thousands of CDS and CD-ROMs with 50% of the net profits going to member nonprofits. (See **<http:www.netbenefit.com/Net/Benefit>**.)

Consumers can choose which nonprofit receives the net profits from their purchases.

There are a few large Internet online services like America Online and CompuServe who have created areas where nonprofit organizations can reside and share information with each other and the public, as well as look for donations—for a price.

America OnLine has created **Accesspoint Civic Involvement System**—a comprehensive online charity center. Citizens can read about the charity sector and they can donate to charities in the village.

There is also an area where charities can post volunteer opportunities.

Charities can post employment or volunteer opportunities on their own site or in a landlord's bulletin board—like AOL's Accesspoint. There are close to 800,000 paying members on AOL and some of them will visit the volunteer opportunity area.

There is also an opportunity to get gifts-in-kind.

The Charity Village in Canada is a diverse charity Internet site that has created a gifts-in-kind Flea Market where it costs commercial organizations, or private citizens, less than $10 U.S. per month to post their products. It's free for charities. (See **<http://www.hilborn.com/cvhome.html>**.)

Nurturing the relationship

Just like other fundraising channels, the Internet demands every charity begin a caring, attentive relationship with the online donor.

When someone begins an online relationship by donating through the Internet or asking for more information, it is contingent on the charity to have an Internet relationship strategy. The e-mail database should be used to nurture a strong, committed relationship into the future.

The opportunity to send e-mail to thousands of people for the cost of a staff member's time—remember, there's no postage or paper—is a fundraising and communication opportunity that can't be missed.

The WWW is intimate, multisensory, rich in information, virtual, real-time, interactive, and communal. Is this good for fundraising? You bet it is! But nonprofit organizations need to take full advantage of its qualities.

Fully utilized with sound and video and live meetings, the Internet can actually bring back some of the real-time, face-to-face opportunities in nonprofit fundraising.

Imagine: instead of telling your story through the mail or a telephone, you'll be able to have a client talk through video. That's a very powerful way to tell your story and the technology is already here to do that.

Conclusion

With every citizen expected to have an e-mail address by the year 2004 (*Utne Reader*, March-April '95 issue), the Internet is not a fad, nor is it the future. It is now!

There are as many fundraising opportunities on the Internet with:

>>> direct donations

>>> exclusive membership areas

>>> corporate sponsorship and advertising

>>> selling products

>>> games of chance

>>> volunteer recruitment

>>> gathering gifts-in-kind

as there are in the "real world."

The direct donations are very small right now, but almost every charity that is online has told me that they expect a steady growth in gifts. They are all happy to wait for their current investment to pay off handsomely in the longterm.

But the charitable sector can't expect this new medium to have a healthy growth period, unless charities agree to have rigorous evaluation mechanisms that measure the success or failure of fundraising endeavors on the Internet.

Like so many other fundraising channels, charities rely on comparative statistics to help them avoid costly errors—especially in a new medium.

And though the Internet is relatively new, it will soon become as cluttered and hyper-competitive as the other fundraising channels.

That means charities have to invest in research and development on the Internet if they want to be well positioned for the future. It is time to act instead of engaging in the short-term thinking that inhibits the success of so many charities.

Considering the low cost and the large and growing potential audience of this new medium, there is now a window of opportunity to make some valuable long-term decisions and investments.

I think it is appropriate to remember what U.K. fundraiser Ken Burnett said in his book, *Relationship Fundraising*:

> **"The future, as always, will belong to the innovator and to those who are close behind."**

An earlier version of this article appeared in the September 1995 issue of the U.K. magazine, Professional Fundraising, *and the November 1995 issue of* The NonProfit Times. *The text was revised in February 1996. Reprinted with permission. Copyright © 1996 Hewitt and Johnston Consultants, 308 Garden Avenue, Toronto, Ontario M6R 1J6, Canada, phone (416) 588-7780, fax (416) 588-7156, e-mail <hjc@io.org>, Web site <http://www.io.org/~hjc/index.html>.*

>>>

5

What you already know about raising money online!

by MAL WARWICK

Yes! Believe it or not, it *is* possible to raise money on the Internet. Not only that, but:

>>> Within a few years, you'll take that for granted. And:

>>> If you've successfully raised money by mail or telephone, you'll have a head start in figuring out how to use e-mail and the Internet.

Those are my three premises. But I don't intend to address the first two of those three points here. Nick Allen, Michael Johnston, and Robbin Zeff have tackled that challenge quite handily elsewhere in this book. Instead, on the following pages, I'll try to demonstrate how easy it is for you to "translate" the techniques of direct mail and telephone fundraising to this exciting new electronic medium.

OK, maybe we won't always refer to "e-mail" or "the Internet." Maybe the ways we access these electronic communications channels will be very different in just a few years—something more closely resembling TV or a picture phone than a desktop computer. But, call it what you will, barring some unforseen catastrophe, you and many of your donors will be communicating electronically—*with each other*—a lot sooner than you might think.

And I'm confident both you and your donors—or, more likely, your donors' children and grandchildren—will find the depth, flexibility, and speed of electronic communications make it easier to build mutually rewarding relationships.

Yes, I said "easier." Just watch how the customized information management possibilities of the World Wide Web will make it easy for you to adapt the techniques and conventions of direct mail fundraising to fundraising online. Who knows—I may even persuade you that the Internet is far and away the most exciting direct response medium ever created!

And if maintaining and updating a World Wide Web page doesn't fit your organization's budget just now, you can begin by using e-mail to expand your relationship with your donors into a new dimension.

Let's start there.

Two ways e-mail can cut your costs and make some of your donors happier

You've got e-mail, right? Six months ago—or a year, or six years—your organization's office manager or someone on the board decided it was time you started getting ready for the 21ˢᵗ Century. Ever since then, you and your colleagues have been networked electronically: You're able to exchange e-mail messages with one another—and maybe with the outside world.

You may not even use this capability very often—no matter. It's there. And if you're in that shrinking minority of active nonprofit organizations without e-mail capability of any sort, the oversight is easily (and cheaply) corrected.

Like the fax in the mid-1980s, E-mail has become an almost indispensable communications tool virtually overnight in the mid-1990s.

And chances are your in-house e-mail system is wired into the global Internet. If your organization has multiple offices, or field staff on the road, the office manager, network administrator, or computer consultant has probably already hooked you up. If not, that doesn't matter much, either. You're only a hop, skip, and a jump away from the Net—and the cost of the connection is dropping on almost a daily basis. The simplest setup requires only a computer, a modem, and one of those ubiquitous free diskettes America Online and CompuServe are flooding into homes and offices all across the United States.

Here, then, are two simple ways your organization can use that capability, tapping the power of the Internet to lower administrative costs and enrich your relationships with your donors.

Fielding inquiries online

Right now, nonprofits generally respond to inquiries—whether from donors or from the general public—in one of two ways:

>>> The telephone rings. You answer it. Or, rather, the receptionist or a volunteer or some other entry-level person takes the call because you're too busy. And, unless your organization has an efficient inquiry-handling system in place, there may be no record of the call. Not only that, but there's no telling what questions were asked—or how they were answered (perhaps even misleadingly). And, with voice-mail and telephone systems being what they are, this person-to-person approach may come across as anything but warm and fuzzy.

>>> A letter arrives—or a note scribbled in the margin of the response device in a direct mail appeal. Assuming this inquiry isn't lost in one of the nooks and crannies of your mailroom or check-processing vendor, someone—probably that same receptionist or volunteer— stuffs a brochure into an envelope and drops it into the mail in

response. In the ideal case, there's also a form letter included in the response—possibly even hand-signed. If distributing information is a big part of your organization's work, there may be multiple publications and several form letters, or even a partially automated system that dispenses "personalized" (computer-generated) letters.

In either case, the response is probably perfunctory—and, unless there's some charge for the information you're sending, there's rarely follow-up action.

Enter e-mail "auto-replies" (see Chapter 3).

For that growing minority of your donors (and the general public) who prefer e-mail to surface mail or the telephone, you can set up one—or many—auto-replies to answer what computer mavens are fond of calling FAQs (frequently asked questions).

For example, a general information line—the equivalent of your generic brochure—can be addressed something like <info@yourorg.org>. Whenever anyone sends an e-mail message to that address, your "server" (that's a computer to us pedestrians) will *automatically* record the inquiry—including the e-mail return address—and reply with the electronic "brochure" you've prepared.

If your organization operates, say, three different active programs, you might establish an auto-reply for each of them. Thus, a donor who writes to <domestic@yourorg.org> will receive information only about your organization's work within your country, while an inquiry directed to <international@yourorg.org> will call up background material on your overseas program efforts.

In either case, this information may be regularly updated—on even a daily basis, if desirable. Or you could maintain a specialized auto-reply address for only a limited time—if, for example, you're providing information about a current emergency or a campaign that's soon to end.

A very few of the virtually limitless possibilities for e-mail auto-replies include:

>>> Information about upcoming events (<events@yourorg.org>)—with a response mechanism to reserve tickets or a table

>>> Detailed background information on the project described in your current direct mail appeal or newsletter (<indepth@yourorg.org>)

>>> Brief biographies of staff members (<staff@yourorg.org>)

Naturally, no one will write to these e-mail addresses unless you publicize them. You'll *want* to do that, however, if you view fundraising as a relationship-building process: You're seeking every possible opportunity to deepen those relationships. And some—a fast-growing number—of your donors will enthusiastically welcome the in-depth information you're providing *at virtually no cost to your organization.*

All it takes is a brief notation along the following lines on an invitation to your next event or at the conclusion of a newsletter article:

"Want to know more? E-mail <indepth@yourorg.org>."

If that doesn't sound simple to you, talk to the nearest computer maven. It's a piece of cake. (Just be sure that, or the majority of your donors not yet online, you provide an accessible alternative!)

Using a similar device, a "list-serv" (see Chapter 3), is slightly more demanding—but potentially even more rewarding for your organization.

Information at your donors' fingertips

Let's say a substantial number of your donors have indicated over the years a passionate—or at least an abiding—interest in your domestic programs. Despite their interest—and, for a great many of them, ready access to e-mail—they may be too busy (or too timid) to seek out in-depth information by e-mailing your auto-reply, <domestic@yourorg.org>.

With a list-serv (or "infobot"), you can broaden donor participation without any hassle to your donors. For any who sign up for the service, you can *automatically send them* that in-depth information on either a regularly scheduled basis or on occasion as new data comes to light.

Setting up a list-serv isn't nearly as complex or as high-tech as it may sound. However, it does demand care and feeding. Much of the work—including all of the "mailing"—can be automated, but somebody has to keep the information up-to-date, maintain the mailing list, trouble-shoot, and answer inquiries (possibly including such questions as "My computer's in the box—what do I do to make it work?").

Interested? If you don't have the technical expertise at hand, give the folks at IGC a call. (Check the back of this book for information on how to contact them.)

Now let's turn to the broader topic of online fundraising—mostly involving the Internet's World Wide Web. Admittedly, much of this isn't quite so simple, and may not yet be practical, especially for groups with limited budgets or small constituencies. However, technically demanding or not, online fundraising techniques must inevitably borrow a great deal from the large body of accumulated knowledge about direct mail, telephone, and broadcast fundraising.

The technologies are new. Most of the rules will prove to be largely the same. (Yes, you may quote me on that.)

The seven basic principles of direct response fundraising

As you'll see very quickly, many of these principles apply to e-mail as well as so-called "snail mail"—and they *all* apply to the Internet—only more so, in some cases!

1. Building relationships

For decades now, direct mail fundraising hasn't been a way to make a quick buck. And I can guarantee the same will be true of e-mail and the Web. These tools are useful over the years in a *long-term development process*—a relationship-building process. Don't expect quick results from online fundraising any more than you can from direct mail or special events.

2. Donor benefits

Donors want to know what's in it for them. They don't respond to your "needs." If you think they do, you're kidding yourself.

Your donors open your envelopes or stay on the phone or control the urge to channel-surf because they perceive you'll show them how to accomplish something (and even, perhaps, to receive something tangible in the process). The same is doubly true in the fast-moving, razzle-dazzle world of the Web—especially with today's younger (and congenitally skeptical) donors. Merely to get a donor's attention, you'll have to show her she'll derive some benefit from the process.

3. Ask for money

The fundraiser's Prime Directive is to ask for money. This is just as true on the Internet as it is in today's more traditional direct response fundraising efforts.

Remember those words: "Ask for Money." It's not enough to "lend your support" or "consider a contribution." We're talking folding money here!

4. Audience of one

One person at a time reads a letter or answers a telephone. Okay, so we might watch TV or listen to the radio among friends or family. But bear with me here: Your message arrives through *individual* sets of eyes or ears. The same is true on the Internet. Anyway, two people just can't be comfortable for very long sitting together at a keyboard!

5. Make it easy to give

Effective direct mail includes a "user-friendly" response device that practically fills itself out. Telemarketing demands immediate followup with a similar device sent by mail. And today's broadcast fundraising requires accessible, round-the-clock, toll-free numbers. With the ability to reply via e-mail at the flick of a finger, your donors can find the Net even friendlier—but only if you design your communications with this in mind.

6. Test!

What makes direct response unique among advertising media is that its results are *measurable*. Given a large enough pool of donors or prospects, you can test just about anything. (In fact, without even half trying, you can acquire all sorts of useless misinformation and spend your organization into oblivion!)

On the Web, testing can be not just extensive but, sometimes, virtually immediate as well. I can't claim to have figured out all the ins and outs and protocols of measuring response on the Internet, but this much is certain: Strip away the bells and whistles, and you'll find that my computer, and yours, are just overpriced counting machines. And, if they can count, they can measure one quantity against another!

Remember: the whole concept of "split testing" came from the world of space advertising. (In split testing, or "A/B testing," response to two statistically equivalent segments or "panels" is compared.) This was long before direct mail as we know it today was developed to sell magazine subscriptions and insurance policies. The original "split tests" were "split runs" of periodicals, with half the print run including version A and the other half featuring version B.

If the *St. Louis Post-Dispatch* could do that in the 1920s, you can bet the *San Jose Mercury Online* can make it work in the 90s!

7. *Don't get carried away!*

Direct mail and telephone fundraising are just two components of the funding and communications mix. The same will be true of e-mail and the Internet—for a long time to come.

In other words, our lives as fundraisers aren't going to get any simpler—not soon, anyway. Direct mail and the telephone aren't going away. Most of us fundraisers will have to keep on doing the things we're already doing—and learn how to function in the new electronic media, too!

These principles can be readily "translated" from today's direct response media to the new world of electronic communications. Let's see how that might work, using practical, real-world examples.

File   Edit   View   Navigate   Tools   Personal Favorites   Help

Give Some **Hope**   *Give Some* **Time**

Give Some **Thought**

[Memorial or Honor Donation Form] [Volunteering with the ACS]
[How Your Contribution Helps]

Guest Book   What's New?   Return   More Info

[Guest Book | What's New | Return | More Info]

The American Cancer Society has gone online with this engaging invitation for help. In some ways, it's like direct mail—but look how many more choices you've got here than you'd find in a typical letter solicitation!

"Translating" direct mail into bits and bytes

"Surveys"

Surveys are a favored direct mail device to involve donors. (Most of the time, it's more accurate to speak of "so-called surveys"—and sneer when you say it. These "surveys" are typically never tallied.) Questionnaires or surveys are especially popular in donor acquisition programs, because they frequently double or triple an otherwise meager response.

Surveys already play an even larger role on the Web—and they needn't be phony! Why? Because ever more sophisticated donors are demanding *real* involvement in the affairs of the causes and institutions they support. And it's much easier to deliver and analyze a survey online.

Remember: Your donors will do the data entry!

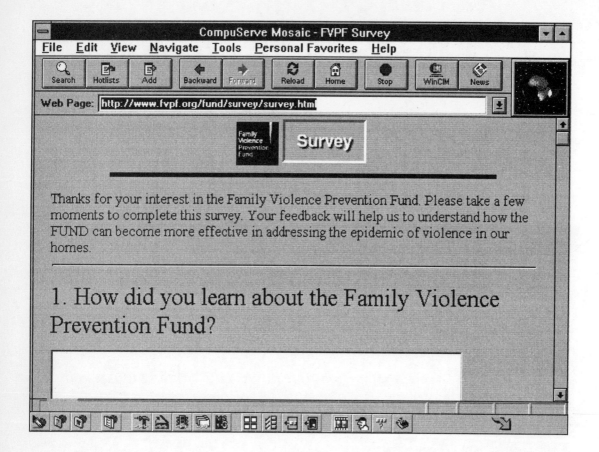

Think how much more useful information the Family Violence Prevention Fund (**<http://www.fvpf.org>**)will derive from this online survey than Wildlife Forever will get from the direct mail "survey" in the donor acquisition package pictured here. (Can't imagine without seeing more of the Family Violence survey? Take another look at the World Wildlife Fund survey you saw in Chapter 2, "Anatomy of a Web site.")

8. Do you participate in local, state or national habitat conservation projects?

☐ Yes
☐ No

9. Do you know of any areas where wildlife habitats need protection or restoration? If so, please list specific areas below:

_____

_____

10. Will you help Wildlife Forever save wildlife habitat by making a tax-deductible membership contribution?

☐ Yes, I want to help
☐ No, I'm unable to help at this time

If you answered "Yes" to the last question, please complete your Membership Acceptance Form below. Thank you.

MEMBERSHIP ACCEPTANCE FORM

☐ **YES, I accept your invitation to become a member of Wildlife Forever at your special introductory rate.** I want to help conserve North America's wildlife by supporting your habitat conservation and restoration projects. Please enroll me in the following membership category:

☐ **$20** Introductory Member
☐ **$25** Regular Member
☐ **$35** Contributing Member
☐ **$50** Habitat Protector
☐ **$100** Wildlife Guardian
☐ $_____

As a new member of Wildlife Forever, you'll receive:

1. A pewter Wildlife Forever key chain.

2. Your FREE subscription to the *Call of the Wild* quarterly newsletter.

3. Your personal Wildlife Forever membership card.

4. Regular updates

Directories

Anything that involves an exchange of information between you and your members or donors can be handled more efficiently—and far more cheaply—via e-mail or the Internet than by mail or phone.

Projects like this University of Michigan alumni directory will be a snap once e-mail is universally accepted. Meanwhile, note that this questionnaire asks for e-mail addresses. You should, too!

THAN

6 PREFERRED .

AB '63

7 RESIDENCE ADDRESS (LINE

2..~ A. ~v P.

8 RESIDENCE ADDRESS (LINE 2)

9 RESIDENCE ADDRESS (LINE 3)

10 CITY

Berkeley

11 STATE	12 ZIP CODE	13 COUNTRY
CA	947..	

14 RESIDENCE PHONE	15 RESIDENCE FAX
51C.5.. ..	

16 RESIDENCE E-MAIL ADDRESS	16 .

17 PROFESSIONAL TITLE OR POSITION WITH FIRM	17 PROFESSION.
18 FIRM NAME	18 FIRM NAME
19 BUSINESS ADDRESS (LINE 1)	19 BUSINESS ADDRESS (LINE 1)
20 BUSINESS ADDRESS (LINE 2)	20 BUSINESS ADDRESS (LINE 2)
21 BUSINESS ADDRESS (LINE 3)	21 BUSINESS ADDRESS (LINE 3)
22 CITY	22 CITY

23 STATE	24 ZIP CODE	25 COUNTRY	23 STATE	24 ZIP CODE	25 COUNTRY

26 BUSINESS PHONE	27 BUSINESS FAX	26 BUSINESS PHONE	27 BUSINESS FAX

28 BUSINESS E-MAIL ADDRESS	28 BUSINESS E-MAIL ADDRESS

29 OCCUPATION CODE	29 OCCUPATION CODE CHOOSE ONE FROM LIST ON BACK OF FORM AND PLACE HERE: ➝

30 MATCHING GIFT COMPANY?	31 PREFERRED ADDRESS FOR U OF M MAILINGS	30 MATCHING GIFT COMPANY? ❑ YES ❑ NO	31 PREFERRED ADDRESS FOR THE ALUMNI ASSOCIATION OF THE UNIVERSITY OF MICHIGAN MAILINGS: ❑ RESIDENCE ❑ BUSINESS

H

100th Anniversary Edition

First-Ever ALL*-University of Michigan Alumni Directory
(*includes BOTH Members & Non-Members of the Alumni Association.)

❑ **HARDBOUND DIRECTORY - Vol.1**   **$39.95**
Plus $6.95 Shipping & Handling
Texas Residents add 6.25% sales tax ($2.93)
Volume 1 lists alumni alphabetically and includes home and business addresses, telephone and fax numbers, and e-mail addresses.

❑ **HARDBOUND DIRECTORIES - Vol. 1 & 2**   **$59.95**
Plus $9.95 Shipping & Handling
Texas Residents add 6.25% sales tax ($4.37)
Includes **Volume 1 and Volume 2** which lists alumni in three additional sections: by class year, by geographic location (with occupation code noted), and by e-mail address.

❑ **CD-ROM DIRECTORY**   **$59.95**
Plus $6.95 Shipping & Handling
Texas Residents add 6.25% sales tax ($4.18)
Includes all of the information available in both printed volumes.

Save $20 - Order Both Volumes and the CD-ROM version.

❑ **HARDBOUND DIRECTORIES - Vol. 1 & 2**   **$99.90**
AND THE CD-ROM DIRECTORY
Plus $9.95 Shipping & Handling
Texas residents add 6.25% sales tax ($6.87)

❑ **Check** payable to University of Michigan Alumni Directory is enclosed.
★*BE SURE TO INCLUDE SHIPPING & HANDLING*★

❑ **Charge** my 1997 University of Michigan Alumni Directory to:

❑ American Express   ❑ Discover   ❑ MasterCard   ❑ VISA

ACCOUNT NUMBER   EXP. DATE

X _____
SIGNATURE FOR CREDIT CARD USE ONLY

CREDIT CARD BILLING WILL APPEAR ON STATEMENT: ALUMNI DIRECTORY PUBLICATIONS, DALLAS, TX

0000831189, Warwick

Publication : Spring 1997

Donor involvement

Get ready for confession or prayer sessions on the Web! Or how about logging on to download the Prayer of the Day? Or to engage in a live online chat with your favorite evangelist?

Crude direct mail donor involvement devices like this one from Our Lady of Lourdes Grotto of the Southwest (see opposite page) will give way over time to more meaningful interaction online—in religion, in science, and in every other conceivable arena of human activity.

Consider, for example, The Nature Conservancy's online offer (**<http:// www.tnc.org>**) of a free screen-saver. It's tough to imagine how a direct mail package could be more involving than this!

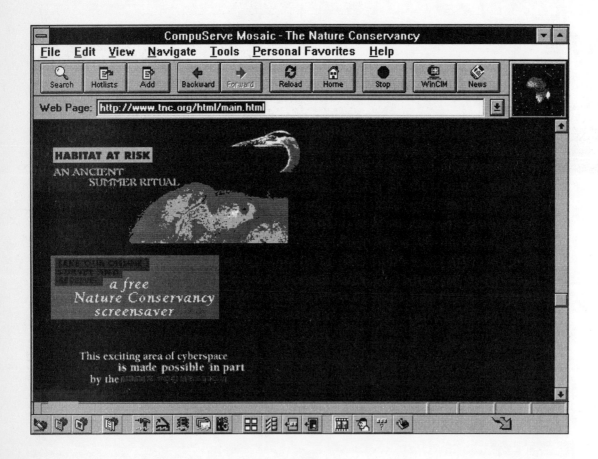

Monthly giving

Direct mail veterans know that monthly giving programs are cumbersome at best when they're limited to paper transactions. An even bigger problem: "fulfillment"—the percentage of gifts pledged that are actually received—is unreliably low with a manual sustainer program. Nowadays, as a result, almost every well-managed monthly pledge or sustainer program is gravitating toward automatic, paperless transactions via credit cards or Electronic Funds Transfer (EFT). In fact, many programs operate exclusively this way, offering no option for donors to mail checks in payment for their pledges—because fulfillment is dramatically better with paperless methods.

Such arrangements are even easier to make and sustain on the Internet. And a single click of the mouse can give the donor a peek at the benefits that come from any given level of monthly support. It's even easy to offer free access to a so-called "applet"—software that performs a very specialized function—through your Web site. One such applet might calculate the total value over time of a donor's monthly gifts at different levels—or even build in an inflation factor. (Remember: Computers don't just do graphics and text! They can figure out stuff on the fly for you or your donors.)

```
┌──────────────────────────────────────────────────────────────────────┐
│ ─                 CompuServe Mosaic - Donations Form            ▼ ▲ │
│  File   Edit   View   Navigate   Tools   Personal Favorites   Help    │
│ ┌────┐ ┌────┐ ┌────┐  ┌────┐ ┌────┐ ┌────┐ ┌────┐ ┌────┐ ┌────┐ ┌────┐│
│ │ Q  │ │    │ │    │  │ ←  │ │ →  │ │ ↻  │ │ ⌂  │ │ ●  │ │    │ │    ││
│ │Search││Hotlists││Add│  │Backward││Forward││Reload││Home ││Stop ││WinCIM││News ││
│ └────┘ └────┘ └────┘  └────┘ └────┘ └────┘ └────┘ └────┘ └────┘ └────┘│
│ Web Page: │http://www.aidsquilt.org/cgi-bin/donorform.cgi        │ ↓  │
│ ┌──────────────────────────────────────────────────────────────┐  ↑ │
│ │ Please enroll me as a Friend of the Quilt at the following level:│  │
│ │                                                                │  │
│ │          ○  Benefactor's Circle  ($2500 or pledge $250/month)  │  │
│ │          ○  Conservator's Circle ($1000 or pledge $100/month)  │  │
│ │          ○  Quilter's Circle ($500-$999 or pledge $50/month)   │  │
│ │          ○  Twelve-by-Twelve Sponsor's Circle                  │  │
│ │             ($250-$499 or pledge $25/month)                    │  │
│ │          ○  Panel Sponsor's Circle ($100-$249 or pledge $10/month)│ │
│ │          ○  Friend's Circle ($35-$99 or pledge $5/month)       │  │
│ │                                                                │  │
│ │ I would like to make a gift of: │          │                   │  │
│ │                                                                │  │
│ │ I would like to make my gift a monthly pledge of: │        │   │  │
│ │                                                                │  │
│ │ Please list my gift in memory of: │              │            │  │
│ │                                                                │  │
│ │ My company has a matching gift program:                        │ ↓ │
│ └──────────────────────────────────────────────────────────────┘    │
└──────────────────────────────────────────────────────────────────────┘
```

The Names Project Donations Form (<http://www.aidsquilt.org>) illustrated on the previous page is an underdeveloped example of online fundraising potential. (No applets here!) But what will we find on The Names Project's Web site in six months, or a year?

By contrast, the Oxfam Canada response device depicted below is about as clear and dramatic as you can get in direct mail.

yes!
War's children must receive care ... they are our children too.

OXFAM NATIONAL OFFICE
251 LAURIER AVE. W. OTTAWA, ONT., K1P 5J6

Your donation counts!

$61 will buy seeds and tools so one family can grow enough food to feed themselves.

$122 will buy an engine repair kit for a truck delivering aid supplies

$1000 will drill a well so children have clean drinking water

HARVEY McKINNON PHOTO

Jorge has lost his mother and father ... but he must not lose our commitment to help.

1 I can send this one time gift:

$30 ☐ $61 ☐ $122 ☐ $244 ☐
$500 ☐ $1000 ☐   your choice $_____

VISA ☐   MASTERCARD ☐

CARD NUMBER _____

SIGNATURE _____ EXPIRY _____

A REMINDER Please make your tax deductible cheque payable to Oxfam Canada. Please send it with this form in the envelope provided.

Name _____

Address _____

City _____ Prov. _____ Code _____

Please help us update our records by correcting your address in the space provided above.

2 I can make a Shareplan pledge:

Shareplan donors give powerful help through monthly donations.
I authorize Oxfam Canada to receive the following donation from my:

☐ Bank account on the 1st of each month. (Enclose a sample cheque marked VOID.)
☐ Charge Card account on the 15th of each month.

$15 monthly ☐ $20 monthly ☐
$25 monthly ☐ $_____ other

VISA ☐   MASTERCARD ☐

CARD NUMBER _____

SIGNATURE _____ EXPIRY _____

Donor benefits

Donors often respond best if we dramatize how much a gift of a certain level will accomplish. ("$25 feeds a child for a week, $50 will nourish a whole family)." The depth and versatility of programming on the Internet opens up the possibility of illustrating a gift's impact in as detailed and graphic a way as any donor might wish. And the color and variable typography of the newer online communications will permit us to place as much or as little emphasis as we desire on any particular gift level.

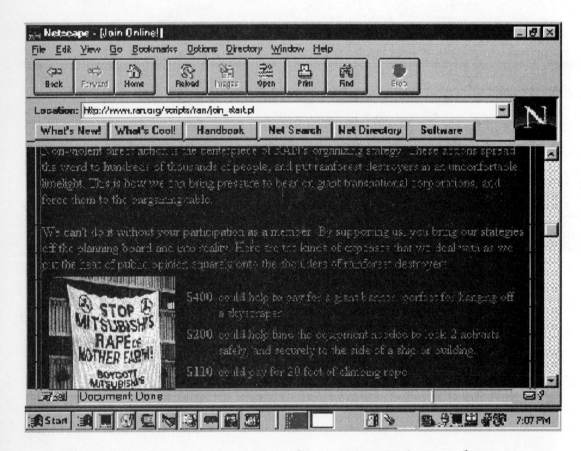

Take the Rainforest Action Network's exciting Web site (**<http://www. ran.org>**), for example. The copy on the screen reads, in part, "$400 could help to pay for a giant banner, perfect for hanging off a skyscraper." Some might not see that as a benefit—but doubtless most Rainforest Action donors and prospects think that banner is an especially attractive reason to join RAN!

In some future of its Web page, RAN might link each of the suggested gift amounts to an illustration of the benefit it brings. Or, instead, they could offer a range of benefits—and link each of them to a pricetag with its own built-in action response device (i.e., a further link to a contribution form, with the amount already filled in).

With that thought in mind, take a look at this typical direct mail response device from Last Chance for Animals:

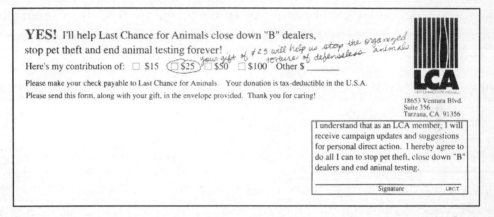

Note also the involvement device in this form—the boxed request for a signature for what many groups call their "action alert network." In direct mail, signature boxes like the one pictured here are included primarily for their involvement value, since they're not a good indication of the individual's willingness or ability to call a Member of Congress or write a letter. (Also, people willing to take such action won't necessarily notice the box.)

Think how much more useful and predictive such a device could be if every respondent were required to *choose* whether or not she would sign up to participate in direct action. You can do that online! But it's tough to make someone check one box or another on a direct mail response device. (What can you do—send it back if a box is left blank?)

Merchandising

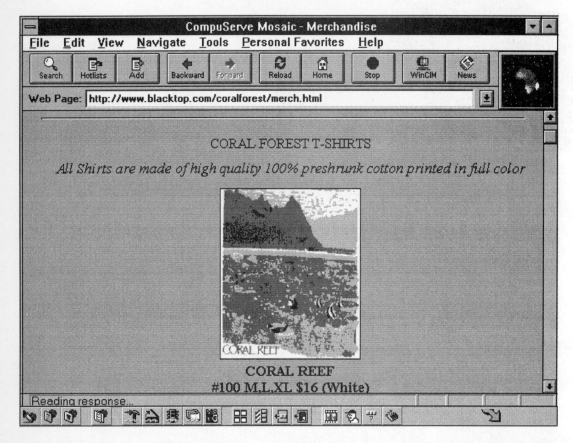

This online T-shirt offer from Coral Forest's Web site (**<http://www. blacktop.com/coralforest/>**) is just a hint of the merchandising potential of the Internet. Soon, merchandising will truly come to life on the Web, with color, live action, and "real-time" (immediate) order entry. And an online catalog can store all the necessary information to make your *next* order even easier—or to suggest other items that may interest you.

Big-time catalog merchants use their own heavy-duty computers to do that now. For most nonprofits such stellar customer service is still out of reach. But not for long!

Meanwhile, most of us make do with direct mail merchandising tools, such as the Whale Adoption Project catalog and order card reproduced on the opposite page.

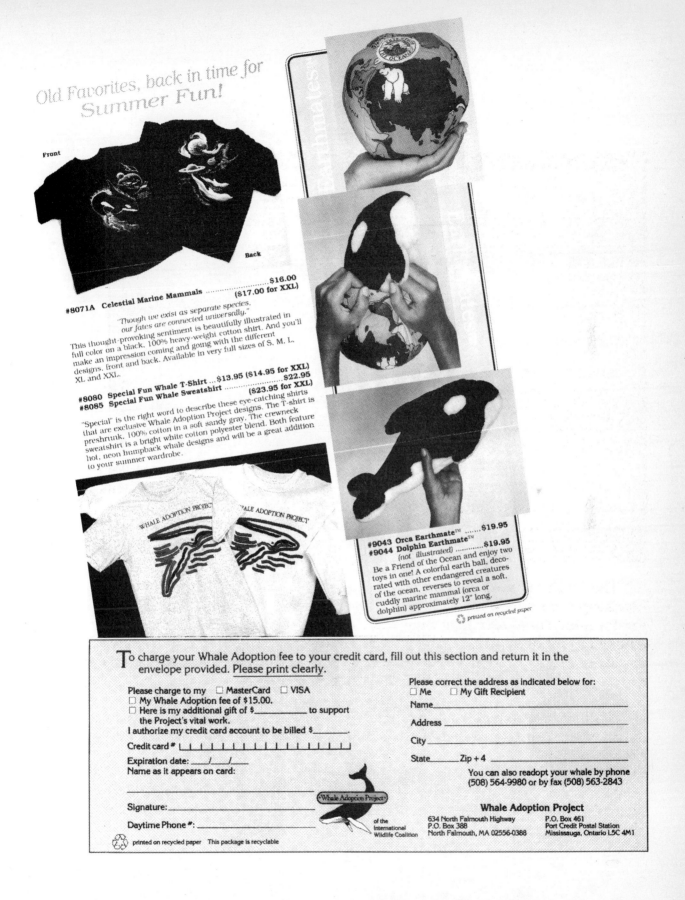

Old Favorites, back in time for Summer Fun!

Front

Back

#8071A Celestial Marine Mammals $16.00
($17.00 for XXL)

*"Though we exist as separate species,
our fates are connected universally."*
This thought-provoking sentiment is beautifully illustrated in full color on a black, 100% heavy-weight cotton shirt. And you'll make an impression coming and going with the different designs, front and back. Available in very full sizes of S, M, L, XL, and XXL.

#8080 Special Fun Whale T-Shirt ...$13.95 ($14.95 for XXL)
#8085 Special Fun Whale Sweatshirt $22.95
($23.95 for XXL)

"Special" is the right word to describe these eye-catching shirts that are exclusive Whale Adoption Project designs. The T-shirt is preshrunk, 100% cotton in a soft sandy gray. The crewneck sweatshirt is a bright white cotton polyester blend. Both feature hot, neon humpback whale designs and will be a great addition to your summer wardrobe.

#9043 Orca Earthmate™ $19.95
#9044 Dolphin Earthmate™ $19.95
(not illustrated)
Be a Friend of the Ocean and enjoy two toys in one! A colorful earth ball, decorated with other endangered creatures of the ocean, reverses to reveal a soft, cuddly marine mammal (orca or dolphin) approximately 12" long.

♻ printed on recycled paper

T o charge your Whale Adoption fee to your credit card, fill out this section and return it in the envelope provided. Please print clearly.

Please charge to my ☐ MasterCard ☐ VISA
☐ My Whale Adoption fee of $15.00.
☐ Here is my additional gift of $_____ to support the Project's vital work.
I authorize my credit card account to be billed $_____.

Credit card # |_|_|_|_|_|_|_|_|_|_|_|_|_|_|_|_|_|_|_|

Expiration date: ___/___/___
Name as it appears on card:

_____

Signature:_____

Daytime Phone #:_____

♻ printed on recycled paper   This package is recyclable

Please correct the address as indicated below for:
☐ Me   ☐ My Gift Recipient
Name_____
Address _____
City _____
State_____ Zip + 4 _____

You can also readopt your whale by phone (508) 564-9980 or by fax (508) 563-2843

Whale Adoption Project
of the International Wildlife Coalition

634 North Falmouth Highway   P.O. Box 461
P.O. Box 388   Port Credit Postal Station
North Falmouth, MA 02556-0388 Mississauga, Ontario L5C 4M1

ACLU Membership Renewal

MY COMMITMENT AS A FORMER
ACLU MEMBER REMAINS FIRM.

AT THIS CRUCIAL TIME, I WANT TO HELP
ACLU BY SETTING MY CONTRIBUTION AT:

( ) $40   ( ) $80
( ) _____

PLEASE CONTINUE MY MEMBERSHIP
THROUGH OCTOBER 1996.

5131113G   CNB   R20938

MAL WARWICK

BERKELEY CA

- To make sure your contribution is properly credited, please return this portion of the form with your check.
- Please make your check payable to ACLU. Contributions to the ACLU are not tax-deductible.
- If you have already sent your payment, please disregard this notice.

(OVER PLEASE)

Recycled Paper

YOUR DUES ARE SHARED WITH THE ACLU OF NORTHERN CALIF

ACLU   132 WEST 43rd STREET   NEW YORK, NEW YORK, 10036-6599

Even the biggest membership renewal or annual giving programs are difficult to administer using only mail and telephone communications. Renewal notices like the one from the ACLU pictured above or that from Amnesty International below are slow to arrive, expensive to process, and drab to the point of boredom. Online systems have the potential to make these transactions easier, faster, and more accurate for both an organization and its members—as well as a lot more interesting.

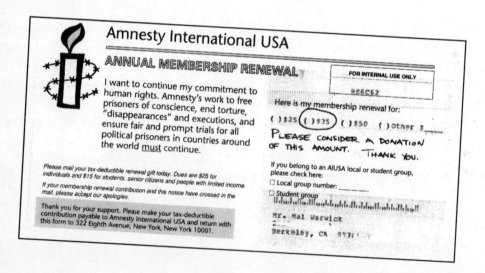

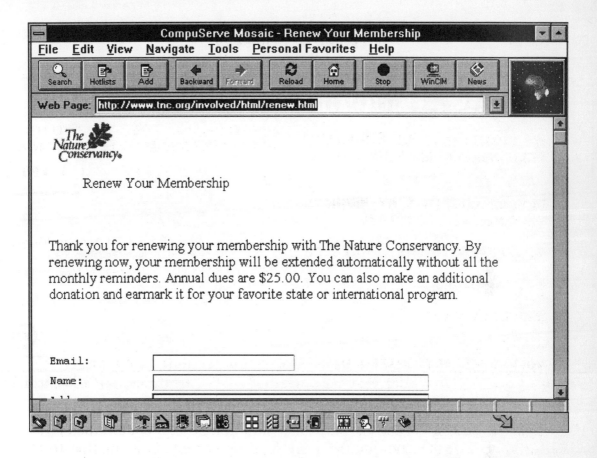

Here, for instance, is The Nature Conservancy's online membership renewal offer. In the page's current form, a member must type in her name, e-mail address, and other information—but how easy it will be to automate that process, making the experience virtually effortless for the member!

And think: No more lost or mislaid renewal notices! No more endless waits for gift acknowledgments or followup mailings! And the process can be *much* more informative for the members on the Web than it is by mail or phone: A click of a mouse could access the highlights of the organization's work during the past year (or ever since the member joined). Or the member's detailed individual giving history might pop up on the screen.

The possibilities seem endless—and that's happening none too fast! Today's donors are demanding better service. Tomorrow's may *expect* all this and more.

Full color, live action

FRIENDS OF THE QUILT

SUPPORTER REPLY

☐ **YES, I want to help the AIDS Memorial Quilt play a unique and powerful role in preventing the spread of AIDS — especially by displaying the Quilt in its entirety in Washington, D.C. in 1996.**

To help The NAMES Project educate Americans about AIDS and prevent more lives from being lost, I am enclosing my contribution of:

☐ $35   ☐ $50   ☐ $75   ☐ $100*   ☐ Other $_____

Members contributing $35 or more receive a one-year subscription to the quarterly *On Display* newsletter, containing information about upcoming Quilt displays and FRIENDS OF THE QUILT activities.

*Gifts of $100 will also be acknowledged with this special 1996 FRIENDS OF THE QUILT membership pin. → →

FRIENDS OF THE QUILT

☐ Check enclosed
☐ Please bill my: ☐ VISA   ☐ MasterCard   ☐ AMEX   ☐ Discover.

Card #_____   Exp. date _____

Cardholder's signature_____

6807   NA35
MR. MAL WARWICK

BERKELEY CA

Please return this form in the enclosed reply envelope to:
The NAMES Project
310 Townsend St., Ste. 310
San Francisco, CA 94107

Contributions to The NAMES Project are tax-deductible as allowed by law.

THE NAMES PROJECT

It's rare to see a full-color response device like this one (reproduced in brilliant, living black-and-white) from a Names Project fundraising appeal—even though many issues or circumstances may cry out for color. On the Web, however, color is the norm. And in the near future, full-motion video will become commonplace as well.

Think how much more dramatic this response device could be if each Names Project supporter could view a brief, full-screen, full-color video of the AIDS Quilt being laid out on the National Mall? Or search the online database to view the section of the Quilt that commemorates a friend or loved one?

To get a sense of these possibilities, look up the Rainforest Action Network Web site again (**<http://www.ran.org>**). From the start, RAN's Internet strategy has been to use leading-edge technologies to dramatize its message—and to attract prospects through curiosity value alone, if necessary. Chairman Man sez check out! And be sure to keep your eyes and ears open when you do.

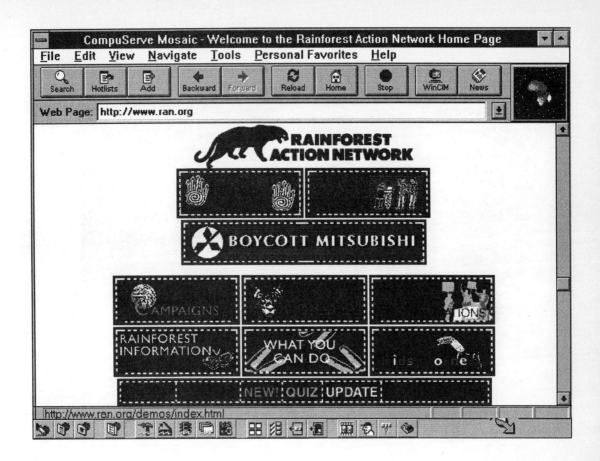

Join over Sixty of the Bay Area's leading performers
for an evening of Musical Theatre, Comedy and Dance!

Celebration for Life

Saturday June 22 1996 8 P.M.

DEAN LESHER
REGIONAL
CENTER
FOR THE ARTS

ALL PROCEEDS TO BENEFIT THE AIDS ALLIANCE
A PRIVATE, NON-PROFIT ORGANIZATION PROVIDING SUPPORT AND EDUCATION
Formerly THE AIDS PROJECT OF CONTRA COSTA and THE CENTER FOR AIDS SERVICES OF ALAMEDA

(510) 943-SHOW
7·4·6·9

Tickets $15, $25, & $35 on sale now at the center ticket office

Bulletins, alerts, and invitations to special events frequently get lost in the clutter of the mailbox. As a result, event organizers are turning more frequently to multiple mailings—"reminders" or "last chance" postcards, for example. Obviously, this postcard mailed by the Dean Lesher Regional Center for the Arts wasn't adequate promotion for the "Celebration for Life." But as a complement to other forms of advertising and promotion, it was useful, no doubt.

With e-mail or the Web, an invitation can not only be repeated as often as the traffic will bear—it can also come with its own, built-in RSVP device! On the opposite page you'll find the Redwood Alliance's online events schedule from its Web page. Because of design limitations, you'll find it hard to read the on screen text in this reproduction. And you won't see the e-mail link to Redwood Alliance built into the notice for this "Bebop & Brew." Just a click of the mouse calls up an e-mail screen pre-addressed to the event's organizers!

Snapshots

We need you to help save tigers in the wild— before it's too late!

Photo © Art Wolfe

WILDLIFE CONSERVATION SOCIETY
BRONX, NEW YORK 10460

T50PCT95

Snapshots of animals or children brighten many direct mail appeals. But full-color photos like the one above from the Wildlife Conservation Society are rarely used in fundraising, because of their high cost. (Few mailers reach the high volumes that lower per-unit printing costs to acceptable levels.)

On a Web site, though, you can post a whole *album* of snapshots —complete with detailed captions and links to information about the work of your organization to save those animals or help those kids! And every snapshot can have its own built-in feedback mechanism: a button that routes the donor directly to the contribution form.

On the Fund for Animals' Web site (<**http://www.envirolink.org/arrs/ fund/>**)—as on countless others—you can get a glimpse of the colorful potential of the Internet to bring the world into our homes.

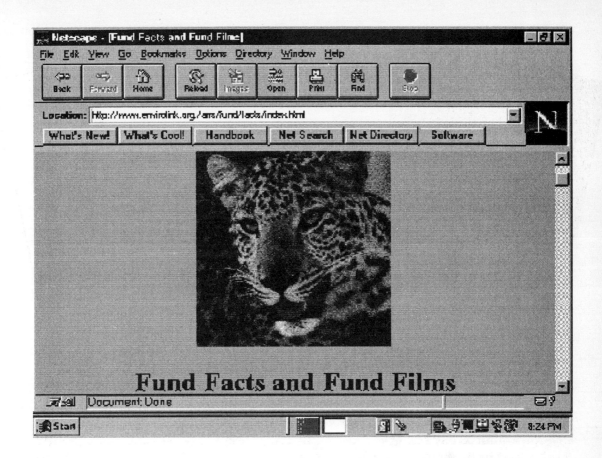

What doesn't "translate" to e-mail and the Net

I hope you've seen in the abundant examples I've used that direct mail techniques really can be readily exported to e-mail and the Internet. But there are differences as well as similarities between the two media—profound differences, in fact.

Two-way communication

In direct response, we humor ourselves with the assertion that direct mail involves a "dialogue." We say that, unlike broadcast advertising, direct mail is a two-way communications channel. And there's a lot of truth to that—certainly as compared to today's television or radio broadcasting. *(I write. I ask. You write back.)*

But there are limits. Direct mail fundraising doesn't really involve two-way communication—at least not anything that the average person on the street would recognize as a conversation. With e-mail and the Internet, however, communications really *does* move back and forth. And it can even involve "real-time" communications, with instantaneous responses.

There are times when the immediacy of communications online can make all the difference in the world. In emergencies, for example. Or in conversations involving illness or injury where instant response may save a life. Or—to cite a more prosaic example—when you're nearing the end of a fundraising campaign and you want to keep donors truly up-to-date with your progress toward a goal.

Frequency

The rules of frequency and timing are fairly well known in direct mail fundraising (even if there's no universal agreement about how they work). For instance, we know that an effective direct mail fundraising program requires year-round communications. And we know a lot about how frequently we can solicit particular groups of donors to maximize their support.

But we know none of these things about fundraising or membership development online. Will donors resent frequent bulletins and alerts—or will they demand them? I have no idea. But I do intend to find out!

"Long letters"

Ever since Tom Collins' and Morris Dees' 12-page letter raised a bundle for George McGovern's 1972 Presidential campaign, direct mail specialists have slugged it out with incredulous nonprofit executives and boards of directors over "long letters." The conventional wisdom in direct mail fundraising is that "the longer the letter, the better the results." Like most conventional wisdom, the statement is faulty: Sometimes it's just not true (though it usually is). But if you think those four-page letters your board complains about are long, you'd better grit your teeth: The volume of information you'll have to shovel onto a Web page will seem like a reference book by comparison!

In direct mail, we reason that few people will actually read every word of a four-page letter. Most will just skim it, and we go to great lengths to make our letters easy to skim (or at least we ought to).

On a well-developed Web site, though, it's almost unthinkable that any individual would read everything we post. A Web site is designed for browsing, thus giving readers a broad range of choices—and the opportunity to read as little as a single phrase or image, or dozens of pages.

Linkages vs. competition

In direct mail fundraising, there've been a few attempts to organize joint campaigns or even "catalogs" of fundraising choices. I've been involved in a couple of these, and, I'm sad to say, they've never panned out.

I think we'll find the opposite is true on the Net. Cooperation will be necessary, because the most cost-effective way to provide the necessary depth of information and build traffic on a Web site is through linkages to other sites.

Today's experiment, tomorrow's commonplace

Now let's take a closer look at the contrast between direct mail and online communications.

For starters, the fundraising package displayed on the following six pages represents the state of the art in direct mail donor involvement today. What's so "involving?" you ask. Here's how a loyal direct mail booster answers that question:

>>> The closed-face (sealed, windowless) outer envelope was addressed to me personally.

>>> The "Commemorative Presidential Print" is, of course, "suitable for framing." In other words, I can do stuff with it.

>>> The letter is addressed to me personally.

>>> So is the lift letter from the President.

>>> My "Certificate of Authenticity" is inscribed personally to me. If I wish, I can do stuff with this, too.

>>> The personalized response device—separated by a perforation from the reply envelope—contains codes suggestive of individual records as well as suggested gift amounts tailored to my previous gifts. And I'm asked to add my signature.

Twenty-five years ago, packages like this one hardly existed. They weren't even theoretically possible in the 1950s—before computers spread to business and the ZIP code was inflicted on an unwilling public. Ironically, packages like this are called "online" packages, because all their components are printed, personalized, trimmed, collated, glued, and bundled for the postal service in one continuous production "line."

1996 PRESIDENTIAL COMMEMORATIVE PRINT

Mal Warwick

ARTWORK ENCLOSED..
PLEASE DO NOT BEND

1996 Commemorative Presidential Print
Presented by President Bill Clinton and the Democratic National Committee

DEMOCRATIC ★ NATIONAL ★ COMMITTEE

Democratic Party Headquarters • 430 South Capitol Street, S.E. • Washington, D.C. 20003

Dear Mal Warwick,

No monarch dictates our laws in the United States. No emperor hands down imperial decrees. We bow to no royalty here. Since its creation over two centuries ago, our nation has been led by individuals who are <u>of</u> the people, chosen <u>by</u> the people, and <u>for</u> the people.

And to remind them of their common origins, our chosen leaders don't live in an oversized palace or an entrenched castle. They live in the White House -- a building that symbolizes the very spirit of democracy in our nation.

Graceful and elegant with its soaring white columns, the White House is a fitting structure for the executive of the most powerful nation on Earth. Yet it remains a home for the President and his family.

Farmers have lived there -- from Thomas Jefferson to Jimmy Carter. Merchants have lived there... attorneys and writers... and many educators. Citizens from all walks of life can still dream that one day, their son or daughter could serve this nation from the Oval Office. As it has been since George Washington laid its cornerstone in 1792, the White House is a beloved symbol of the United States and the democracy we all hold so dear.

To celebrate all that this wonderful house represents, the Democratic National Committee, on behalf of President Bill Clinton and First Lady Hillary Rodham Clinton, commissioned noted Washington, D.C. artist Dan Kessler to produce a special painting of the White House, which has now been produced as the 1996 Presidential Commemorative Print.

This is the second year that the DNC and the Clintons have asked Mr. Kessler to portray the White House. Last year, he produced a beautiful rendering of the building's north front.

This year, Mr. Kessler chose to paint the south portico and the distinctive curve of the "Truman Balcony," added to the White House by President Harry Truman because he so prized the view. From here, presidents have welcomed foreign dignitaries with pomp and diplomacy -- and from here each spring, the President invites the children of America to an Easter egg roll on the lawn.

John Kennedy's children played here. Color guards, marching bands, and military reviews have enhanced special occasions. Kings, queens, and leaders from across the globe have come here to pay their respects to the President and the young and vital country he leads.

over, please

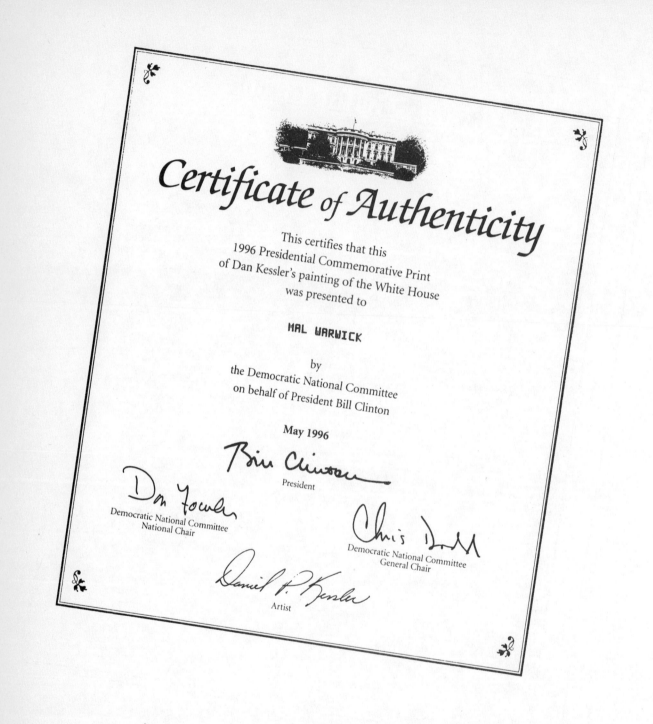

Certificate of Authenticity

This certifies that this
1996 Presidential Commemorative Print
of Dan Kessler's painting of the White House
was presented to

MAL WARWICK

by
the Democratic National Committee
on behalf of President Bill Clinton

May 1996

Bill Clinton
President

Don Fowler
Democratic National Committee
National Chair

Chris Dodd
Democratic National Committee
General Chair

Daniel P. Kessler
Artist

BILL CLINTON

Dear Mal Warwick,

Since Hillary, Chelsea, and I came to this wonderful house almost four years ago, it truly has become our home, and we feel honored and privileged to live here.

That's why we were so pleased when Dan Kessler accepted our invitation to paint the White House again this year. His magnificent painting fills me with much pride -- both for this building, and for our nation.

I want to share this artwork with you as a small "thank you" for the support you've given to me and to my family. Your steadfast and loyal commitment paved the way to the White House for me and the Democratic Party, and your ongoing dedication has kept us strong. So when you look at this print, I hope you will feel the same glow of pride that I feel.

The White House truly is the "house of the people."

Sincerely,

Bill Clinton

Bill Clinton

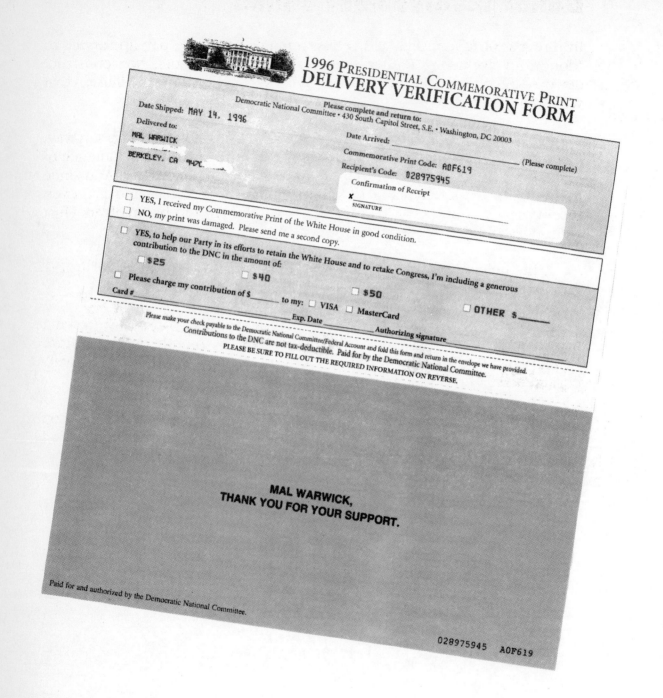

1996 PRESIDENTIAL COMMEMORATIVE PRINT
DELIVERY VERIFICATION FORM

Democratic National Committee

Please complete and return to:
430 South Capitol Street, S.E. • Washington, DC 20003

Date Shipped: MAY 14, 1996

Delivered to:

MAL WARWICK

BERKELEY, CA 9420

Date Arrived: _____

_____ (Please complete)

Commemorative Print Code: AOF619

Recipient's Code: 028975945

Confirmation of Receipt

X _____
SIGNATURE

☐ YES, I received my Commemorative Print of the White House in good condition.

☐ NO, my print was damaged. Please send me a second copy.

☐ YES, to help our Party in its efforts to retain the White House and to retake Congress, I'm including a generous contribution to the DNC in the amount of:

☐ $25   ☐ $40

☐ Please charge my contribution of $_____

☐ $50

Card # _____ to my: ☐ VISA ☐ MasterCard   ☐ OTHER $_____

Exp. Date _____   Authorizing signature _____

Please make your check payable to the Democratic National Committee/Federal Account and fold this form and return in the envelope we have provided.
Contributions to the DNC are not tax-deductible. Paid for by the Democratic National Committee.
PLEASE BE SURE TO FILL OUT THE REQUIRED INFORMATION ON REVERSE.

MAL WARWICK,
THANK YOU FOR YOUR SUPPORT.

Paid for and authorized by the Democratic National Committee.

028975945   AOF619

Donor involvement online

In direct mail fundraising, as I've just reminded you, we pay lip service to "donor involvement." Rather than really involve donors, we construct devices—often transparently pointless devices—to give donors the illusion that we're asking them to do something more than write checks.

But we won't get away with that on the Net—not for long, anyway. Electronic communications can be instantaneous, tailored to an audience of one, and include as much or as little information as is necessary. And since this is *possible*, it won't be long before donors *expect* it—and are even resentful if we don't give it to them. They'll *demand* to be involved. (Just wait: If you haven't seen that yet, you will!)

And the opportunity for genuine, ongoing involvement is really the fundamental difference between online fundraising and direct mail.

By contrast with the direct mail fundraising package you've just viewed, take a look now at the July 1996 appeal of the month on the Nature Conservancy Web site—one of the very best examples of thoughtful, well-designed use of this new medium.

You'll find something much like this when you access **<www.tnc.org>** on the Internet. You'll arrive at The Nature Conservancy's home page. When I clicked on the "Project of the Month," here's what I got:

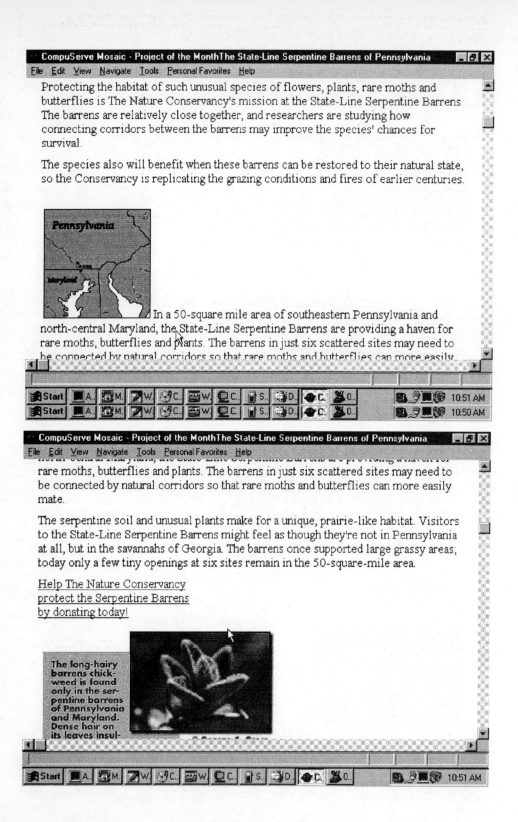

CompuServe Mosaic - Project of the MonthThe State-Line Serpentine Barrens of Pennsylvania

File   Edit   View   Navigate   Tools   Personal Favorites   Help

Protecting the habitat of such unusual species of flowers, plants, rare moths and butterflies is The Nature Conservancy's mission at the State-Line Serpentine Barrens. The barrens are relatively close together, and researchers are studying how connecting corridors between the barrens may improve the species' chances for survival.

The species also will benefit when these barrens can be restored to their natural state, so the Conservancy is replicating the grazing conditions and fires of earlier centuries.

In a 50-square mile area of southeastern Pennsylvania and north-central Maryland, the State-Line Serpentine Barrens are providing a haven for rare moths, butterflies and plants. The barrens in just six scattered sites may need to be connected by natural corridors so that rare moths and butterflies can more easily

CompuServe Mosaic - Project of the MonthThe State-Line Serpentine Barrens of Pennsylvania

File   Edit   View   Navigate   Tools   Personal Favorites   Help

rare moths, butterflies and plants. The barrens in just six scattered sites may need to be connected by natural corridors so that rare moths and butterflies can more easily mate.

The serpentine soil and unusual plants make for a unique, prairie-like habitat. Visitors to the State-Line Serpentine Barrens might feel as though they're not in Pennsylvania at all, but in the savannahs of Georgia. The barrens once supported large grassy areas; today only a few tiny openings at six sites remain in the 50-square-mile area.

Help The Nature Conservancy
protect the Serpentine Barrens
by donating today!

The long-hairy barrens chick-weed is found only in the serpentine barrens of Pennsylvania and Maryland. Dense hair on its leaves insul-

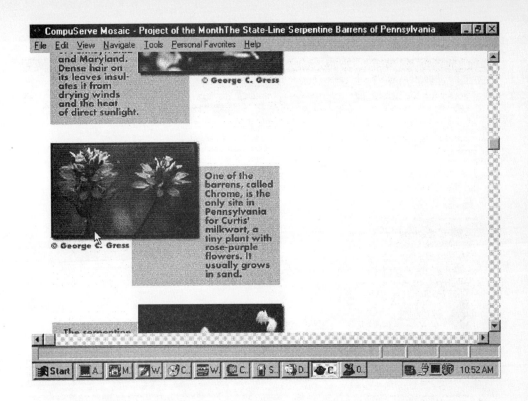

File Edit View Navigate Tools Personal Favorites Help

and Maryland. Dense hair on its leaves insulates it from drying winds and the heat of direct sunlight.

© George C. Gress

One of the barrens, called Chrome, is the only site in Pennsylvania for Curtis' milkwort, a tiny plant with rose-purple flowers. It usually grows in sand.

© George C. Gress

The serpentine

Start A. M. W. C. W. C. S. D. C. O. 10:52 AM

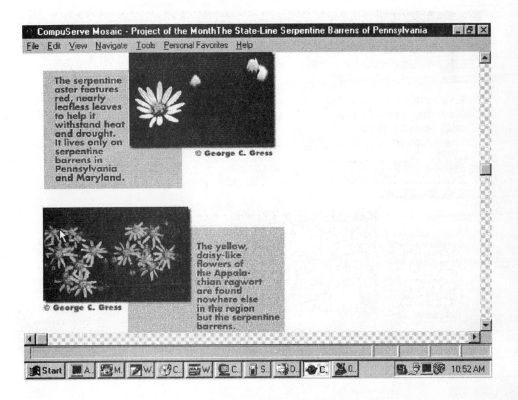

File Edit View Navigate Tools Personal Favorites Help

The serpentine aster features red, nearly leafless leaves to help it withstand heat and drought. It lives only on serpentine barrens in Pennsylvania and Maryland.

© George C. Gress

The yellow, daisy-like flowers of the Appalachian ragwort are found nowhere else in the region but the serpentine barrens.

© George C. Gress

Start A. M. W. C. W. C. S. D. C. O. 10:52 AM

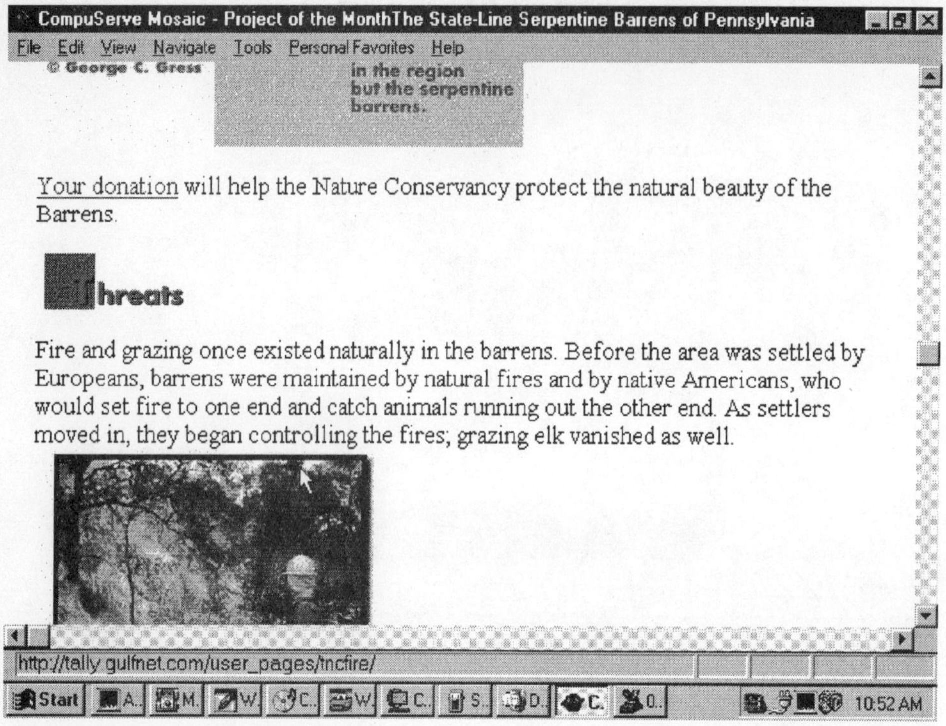

CompuServe Mosaic - Project of the MonthThe State-Line Serpentine Barrens of Pennsylvania

File Edit View Navigate Tools Personal Favorites Help

© George C. Gress

in the region
but the serpentine
barrens.

Your donation will help the Nature Conservancy protect the natural beauty of the Barrens.

Threats

Fire and grazing once existed naturally in the barrens. Before the area was settled by Europeans, barrens were maintained by natural fires and by native Americans, who would set fire to one end and catch animals running out the other end. As settlers moved in, they began controlling the fires; grazing elk vanished as well.

http://tally.gulfnet.com/user_pages/tncfire/

Start A. M. W. C. W. C. S. D. C. 0. 10:52 AM

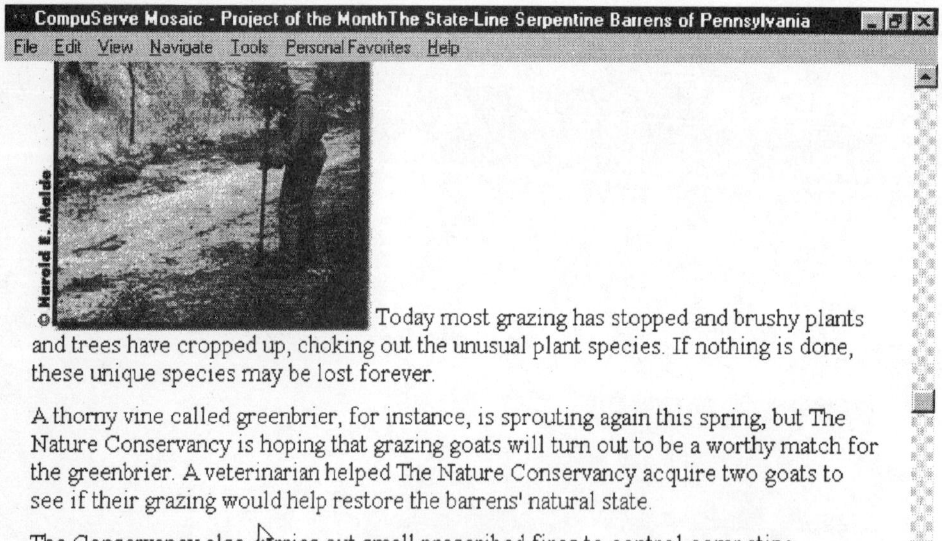

CompuServe Mosaic - Project of the MonthThe State-Line Serpentine Barrens of Pennsylvania

File Edit View Navigate Tools Personal Favorites Help

© Harold E. Malde

Today most grazing has stopped and brushy plants and trees have cropped up, choking out the unusual plant species. If nothing is done, these unique species may be lost forever.

A thorny vine called greenbrier, for instance, is sprouting again this spring, but The Nature Conservancy is hoping that grazing goats will turn out to be a worthy match for the greenbrier. A veterinarian helped The Nature Conservancy acquire two goats to see if their grazing would help restore the barrens' natural state.

The Conservancy also carries out small prescribed fires to control competing vegetation. Without fire, red maple and several other species would invade the barrens.

Start A. M. W. C. W. C. S. D. C. 0. 10:53 AM

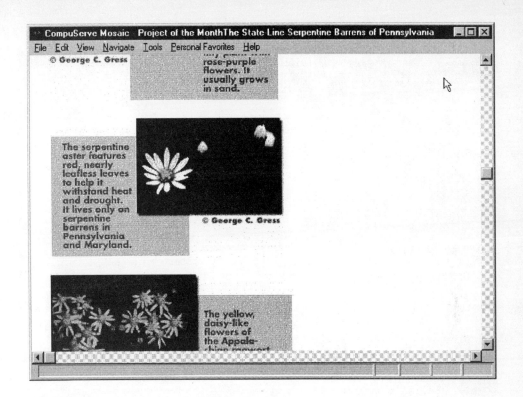

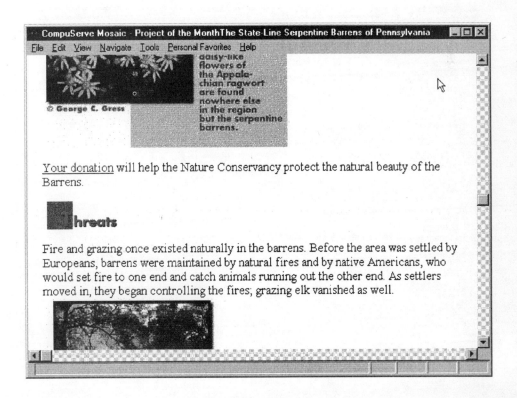

Your donation will help the Nature Conservancy protect the natural beauty of the Barrens.

Threats

Fire and grazing once existed naturally in the barrens. Before the area was settled by Europeans, barrens were maintained by natural fires and by native Americans, who would set fire to one end and catch animals running out the other end. As settlers moved in, they began controlling the fires; grazing elk vanished as well.

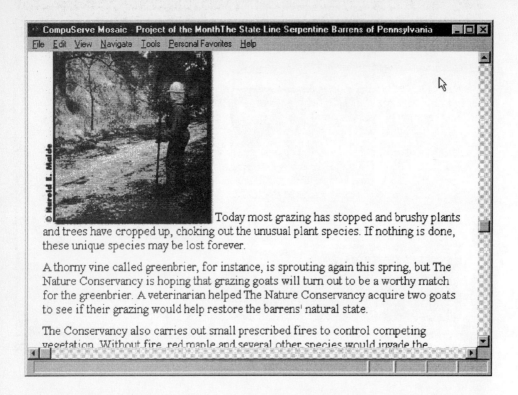

Today most grazing has stopped and brushy plants and trees have cropped up, choking out the unusual plant species. If nothing is done, these unique species may be lost forever.

A thorny vine called greenbrier, for instance, is sprouting again this spring, but The Nature Conservancy is hoping that grazing goats will turn out to be a worthy match for the greenbrier. A veterinarian helped The Nature Conservancy acquire two goats to see if their grazing would help restore the barrens' natural state.

The Conservancy also carries out small prescribed fires to control competing vegetation. Without fire, red maple and several other species would invade the

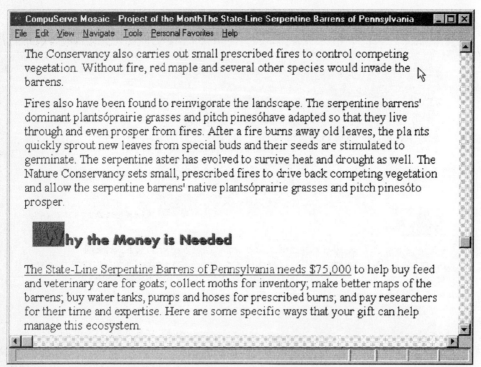

The Conservancy also carries out small prescribed fires to control competing vegetation. Without fire, red maple and several other species would invade the barrens.

Fires also have been found to reinvigorate the landscape. The serpentine barrens' dominant plantsóprairie grasses and pitch pinesóhave adapted so that they live through and even prosper from fires. After a fire burns away old leaves, the pla nts quickly sprout new leaves from special buds and their seeds are stimulated to germinate. The serpentine aster has evolved to survive heat and drought as well. The Nature Conservancy sets small, prescribed fires to drive back competing vegetation and allow the serpentine barrens' native plantsóprairie grasses and pitch pinesóto prosper.

Why the Money is Needed

The State-Line Serpentine Barrens of Pennsylvania needs $75,000 to help buy feed and veterinary care for goats; collect moths for inventory; make better maps of the barrens; buy water tanks, pumps and hoses for prescribed burns; and pay researchers for their time and expertise. Here are some specific ways that your gift can help manage this ecosystem.

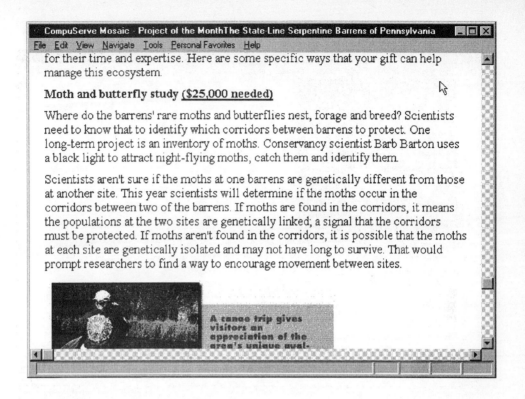

for their time and expertise. Here are some specific ways that your gift can help manage this ecosystem.

Moth and butterfly study ($25,000 needed)

Where do the barrens' rare moths and butterflies nest, forage and breed? Scientists need to know that to identify which corridors between barrens to protect. One long-term project is an inventory of moths. Conservancy scientist Barb Barton uses a black light to attract night-flying moths, catch them and identify them.

Scientists aren't sure if the moths at one barrens are genetically different from those at another site. This year scientists will determine if the moths occur in the corridors between two of the barrens. If moths are found in the corridors, it means the populations at the two sites are genetically linked; a signal that the corridors must be protected. If moths aren't found in the corridors, it is possible that the moths at each site are genetically isolated and may not have long to survive. That would prompt researchers to find a way to encourage movement between sites.

A canoe trip gives visitors an appreciation of the area's unique qual-

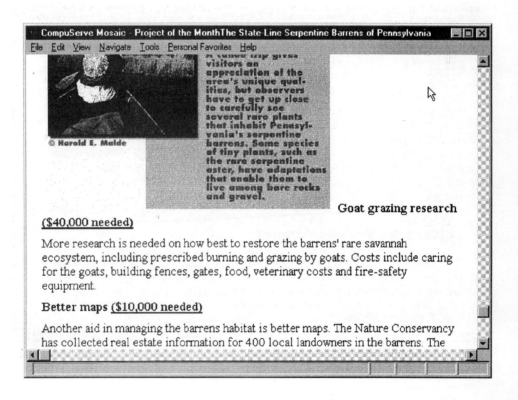

© Harold E. Malde

A canoe trip gives visitors an appreciation of the area's unique qualities, but observers have to get up close to carefully see several rare plants that inhabit Pennsylvania's serpentine barrens. Some species of tiny plants, such as the rare serpentine aster, have adaptations that enable them to live among bare rocks and gravel.

Goat grazing research ($40,000 needed)

More research is needed on how best to restore the barrens' rare savannah ecosystem, including prescribed burning and grazing by goats. Costs include caring for the goats, building fences, gates, food, veterinary costs and fire-safety equipment.

Better maps ($10,000 needed)

Another aid in managing the barrens habitat is better maps. The Nature Conservancy has collected real estate information for 400 local landowners in the barrens. The

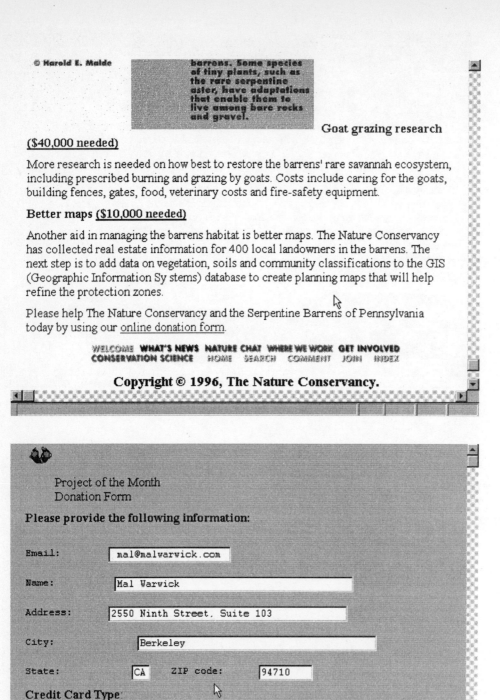

© Harold E. Malde

barrens. Some species of tiny plants, such as the rare serpentine aster, have adaptations that enable them to live among bare rocks and gravel.

Goat grazing research ($40,000 needed)

More research is needed on how best to restore the barrens' rare savannah ecosystem, including prescribed burning and grazing by goats. Costs include caring for the goats, building fences, gates, food, veterinary costs and fire-safety equipment.

Better maps ($10,000 needed)

Another aid in managing the barrens habitat is better maps. The Nature Conservancy has collected real estate information for 400 local landowners in the barrens. The next step is to add data on vegetation, soils and community classifications to the GIS (Geographic Information Sy stems) database to create planning maps that will help refine the protection zones.

Please help The Nature Conservancy and the Serpentine Barrens of Pennsylvania today by using our online donation form.

WELCOME WHAT'S NEWS NATURE CHAT WHERE WE WORK GET INVOLVED
CONSERVATION SCIENCE HOME SEARCH COMMENT JOIN INDEX

Project of the Month
Donation Form

Please provide the following information:

Email: `mal@malwarwick.com`

Name: `Mal Warwick`

Address: `2550 Ninth Street, Suite 103`

City: `Berkeley`

State: `CA` ZIP code: `94710`

Credit Card Type

● MC ○ VISA ○ Amex ○ Discover

Credit Card Number:

Name on the Card: `Mal Warwick`

Credit Card Number:

Name on the Card: Mal Warwick

Expriation Date:

Please enter the amount here:

- ○ $10.00
- ○ $20.00
- ○ $30.00
- ○ $50.00
- ○ $100.00
- ● $250.00
- ○ more

If more, please specify:

May we correspond with you by e-mail?:

- ● Yes
- ○ No
- ○ Other address

If other, please specify:

(Your e-mail address will enable us to save money by sending your

---

○ more

If more, please specify:

May we correspond with you by e-mail?:

- ● Yes
- ○ No
- ○ Other address

If other, please specify:

(Your e-mail address will enable us to save money by sending your confirmation and other correspondence by e-mail rather than regular mail. Thank you for helping us to conserve our natural resources)

Thank you for your support of this important Nature Conservancy initiative.

Send   Start Over

WELCOME WHAT'S NEWS NATURE CHAT WHERE WE WORK GET INVOLVED
CONSERVATION SCIENCE HOME SEARCH COMMENT JOIN INDEX

Copyright © 1996, The Nature Conservancy.

Integrating your online fundraising with other development efforts

Advertising people know the virtues of multichannel communications. One of the first lessons taught in that field is that well-timed, well-coordinated messages conveyed to the same audience through two different media—say, television and direct mail—can be more than twice as effective as sending the same message through only one of these media.

To my enormous gratification, some fundraisers have even figured this out! Occasionally, we'll see a well-executed fundraising campaign that uses direct mail, telephone contact, space advertising, and face-to-face solicitation in combination. When a campaign is "integrated" in this fashion, it can be far more effective than any sequence of separate, uncoordinated solicitations.

We're going to find that's the case with electronic communications, too.

Convergence—or divergence?

You've probably heard or read something about the technological "convergence" of computers, the telephone, and both broadcast and cable television. They're all merging, the theory goes. They'll be replaced by some universal communications network that includes elements of each of them.

Well, there may be some truth to that—in the long run. In fact, I'm convinced that will be the case—eventually. But, as John Maynard Keynes said, in the long run, we're all dead.

For the time being, we would be wise to worry instead about technological *divergence*. Because, instead of replacing direct mail, newspapers, magazines, cable TV, and the telephone, the Internet (or whatever it comes to be called) will simply add one more communications channel to the broad mix already available to us.

Cross-promotion

Your activities on the Internet won't occur in a vacuum—at least they won't succeed all by their lonesome. But think how much cross-promotional value your organization can derive from a newsletter article or an insert in your gift acknowledgment package for any one of the following:

>>> A live, online chat with your executive director

>>> An online briefing from your scientific advisers

>>> The "issue of the month"

>>> An up-to-the-minute bulletin on your campaign's day-by-day progress

>>> An invitation to "get to know your staff"

>>> An "open" board of trustees meeting conducted online

Cross-promotion works both ways, of course! Your direct mail, special events, television coverage, or what-have-you can all be inexpensively promoted—and, eventually, to great effect.

This is where "divergence" comes in mighty handy!

Know your members: past, present, and future

We're already learning a great deal about donors' preferences among solicitation methods.

>>> For instance, we know that resistance to telephone fundraising is strong among older donors. Most of us old folks greatly prefer to be solicited by mail.

>>> Meanwhile, it's becoming progressively clearer that younger donors—say, between 25 and 45—favor the telephone over the mail.

>>> Similarly, older donors tend to be suspicious of Electronic Funds Transfer and credit cards. Good old-fashioned checks will do quite nicely for most of us, thank you (yours truly excepted)!

>>> But younger people are likely to find credit cards more convenient. After all, why not just pass along the card or the number and let someone else do the work?

No one should be surprised, then, when we learn how much more readily the latest generation of donors—the 20-something crowd—takes to giving over the Net. They may have to get a bit older and richer before they can be expected to give generously and frequently. But the evidence is most people under 25 are quite comfortable using computers, e-mail, and the Internet for any purpose whatsoever. There's also plenty of evidence they could turn out to be just as generous as their parents or grandparents. (For example, check out the nationwide statistics for volunteer activities by young people.)

These intergenerational differences are another reason why technological divergence will be the reality for a very long time before convergence takes hold.

Demographics rule!

Other demographic factors will also make a difference. Fundraising has already been turned upside down by the women's movement (even though some fundraisers still seem to be having trouble figuring out that donors can be women!). But just wait! The explosive growth of ethnic "minority" populations in the U.S. will bring changes that are equally dramatic.

Between increased immigration and the higher birth rates common in some ethnic minority communities, the proportion of Caucasians in the U.S. population is shrinking. That won't come as a surprise to anyone in California—or in New York, Toronto, Miami, Chicago, or Vancouver, for that matter!

As fundraisers, we're going to have to understand these influences a whole lot better than most of us do now. For starters, we'll have to be a lot more sensitive than most Americans now are to differences of language . . . to the ways culture affects one's world-view . . . and to the varying roles that culture and religion play in forming our habits and assumptions.

Staying ahead of the game

So, where does this all leave us? Confused? Scared?

That shouldn't be the case. In fact, to my mind, these rapid-fire changes are exciting—I'm one of those weird "early adopters" who actually *likes* change! But I'm also convinced that the growing variety and depth of communications channels means that fundraisers can do a better job of educating, cultivating, and motivating donors.

In other words, I think we're going to come out ahead of the game in the long run.

But everybody won't be so fortunate. Those who have the vision and the determination to wade into these unmapped waters—and devote the time and effort and money necessary to stick it out despite meager early results—these are the people and the organizations that will come out ahead. But some, unfortunately, are going to fall behind. Don't let that be you!

Remember the fundamentals!

One more thing: *don't reinvent the wheel*. Keep the fundamentals of fundraising in mind! And, as you venture into the new possibilities of direct response fundraising and membership development through electronic means, focus on the essential nature of what you're doing.

There's enough magic in the words *direct response.* Whiz-bang technology just gives us new ways to relate to new generations of donors.

Mwosi Swenson conducted much of the research for this chapter.

6

Taking the plunge into e-mail fundraising

by AUDRIE KRAUSE

Editor's note: We received the following letter—via e-mail, of course!—in response to Mal Warwick's March 1996 NonProfit Times *column on "Raising Money by E-mail." As a real-world case study, it's fascinating. But be careful. This article reports on an atypical organization—one that's unusually well attuned to the Information Age. The group's name? Computer Professionals for Social Responsibility. But please don't dismiss this tale out of hand. It won't be all that long before most of your members or donors use e-mail regularly, too!*

I'd been planning a dinner to honor two departing members of our board of directors, as well as celebrate the organization's fifteenth anniversary. Since our members and supporters are primarily people who communicate by e-mail, I decided to include e-mail communications in my fundraising strategy.

In early February, we mailed our initial sponsor letters, using the usual route of the U.S. Postal Service. Normally, this would be followed up by personal calls. However, I decided to include an interim step—sending a follow-up message by e-mail prior to calling. I also made initial contacts by e-mail with a handful of potential corporate sponsors.

Here's what happened:

>>> One corporate sponsor responded in less than 24 hours, purchasing a table of 10 for $1,500. We had not previously solicited contributions from this corporation, by postal mail or telephone!

>>> Several individuals responded affirmatively after being contacted by e-mail.

>>> Eventually, two other corporate sponsors sent word by e-mail that they planned to participate.

Before the actual invitations were mailed, this effort raised approximately $35,000, on a mailing to about 250 potential sponsors.

When the final results were in, the dinner raised in excess of $41,000, drew approximately 200 people, and wound up being the most successful fundraising event in CPSR's 15-year history! Net revenue was over $20,000.

Of course, there were also some declines by e-mail—possibly an easy way out. But overall, I think e-mail was helpful to this fundraising effort.

In addition to adding another contact opportunity between the letter and the follow-up phone call, e-mail eliminated some of the record-keeping associated with the event, since both the outgoing and incoming messages can easily be stored on the computer. It also helped reduce costs by eliminating the need for some long-distance follow-up calls.

The dinner sponsor letter was also posted on our Web page and distributed on our general announcement list, and one individual sponsor was added through these electronic channels.

We mailed the general invitation in early May, and I used e-mail and other electronic distribution channels to follow up that mailing as well.

Since we mailed approximately 1,700 invitations, it was not possible to follow up individually with everyone, either by phone or by e-mail. Before initiating any telephone follow-up, I drafted a personalized follow-up message and used the "cut-and-paste" technique to send individual e-mail messages to targeted names from the invitation list. Again, this resulted in some additional commitments to attend, as well as some declines.

As an additional promotional strategy, I arranged to set up a Web page for testimonials honoring the two guests of honor at the dinner. My hope was that this would motivate some donations from members outside the immediate Bay Area who would not be able to attend.

Initially, testimonials for this web page were solicited via an e-mail announcement to CPSR's list services. The announcement was also posted on the CPSR Web page. Volunteers were recruited to translate the testimonials into Hypertext Markup Language (html) for posting on the Web.

Later, I incorporated the testimonial solicitation into my follow-up to the invitation mailing. Donors who responded to my e-mail message by indicating that they were too far away to attend the dinner received a brief message inviting them to contribute a testimonial to the Web page.

Our organization's experience may not be typical, since our membership is comprised of individuals who have been using e-mail far longer than most people. But it does support the view that e-mail can be a useful enhancement to other ways of communicating with donors.

Audrie Krause is the former Executive Director of Computer Professionals for Social Responsibility and is currently consulting. She can be reached at 601 Van Ness Avenue, San Francisco, CA 94102, phone (415) 775-8674, fax (415) 673-3813, e-mail <akrause@cpsr.org>.

>>>

Web sites useful for fundraisers

by MARTHA SIMPSON

General reference sites for fundraisers

<http://www.clark.net/pub/pwalker>

Nonprofit Resources Catalog, managed by Phillip Walker. This site is an extensive hyperlinked catalog of general resources for nonprofit organizations. From the home page click on "Fundraising and Giving" to access development-related links.

<http://www.duke.edu/~ptavern/Pete.meta-index.html>

The Meta-Index of nonprofit organizations on the Web. Considered by some to be the mother of all sites for nonprofit Internet resources. Formerly managed by Ellen Spertus, and sometimes still referred to as the Spertus List. Liberally peppered with philanthropy-related links.

<http://www.sils.umich.edu/~nesbeitt/nonprofits/nonprofits.html>

Guide to Internet Resources for Nonprofit Public Service Organizations, managed by Sarah Nesbeitt and Richard Truxall. From the home page, click on the "Funding Opportunities" link. Allows keyword searching.

<http://www.umich.edu/~trinket/Resources_for_Grant.html>

Resources for Grantwriters on the Internet. A nice collection of links to fundraising resources collected and annotated by Eva Lyford at the University of Michigan.

<http://www.einet.net/galaxy/Community/Charity-and-Community-Service.html>

This is part of Tradewave's Galaxy, a general directory of resources on the Internet. By going into their Charity and Community Service link I found some interesting odds and ends of things that I hadn't come across anywhere else.

<http://supportcenter.org/sf/>

Beginning in the fall of '96, if you drop by the Support Center's site and click on the nonprofit GENIE's lamp, you can access FAQs (frequently asked questions) on a wide range of fundraising topics. Nationally recognized fundraiser Kim Klein will be among the development luminaries sharing their experiences and advice here.

<http://fdncenter.org>

The Foundation Center site is a bit paradoxical. If you go there thinking you'll be able to search the Center's famous directories of funding sources you'll be disappointed. (For information on those databases see paragraph below.) What you do get when you visit their site is a first-rate collection of links to foundation, corporate, and government funding sites. They also provide advice on proposal writing and funding research, as well as information about the Foundation Center services and publications. You can also access *Philanthropy Digest*, which contains summaries of funding news from around the country.

The Foundation Center's *Foundation Directory* and *Grant Index* are searchable online via Dialog. Fees are $30 per hour for either database, plus a 70¢ per record printing fee. For more information you can contact Dialog at 800-334-2564. The San Francisco Foundation Center recently began offering this fee-for-searching service at its library on Sutter Street. For more information, call (415) 397-0903.

<http://www.accesspt.com/Fundraising/>

This is a new site on the Web and you'll have to pay to use it. AccessPoint, a for-profit company that specializes in nonprofit services, has created databases of foundation and corporate sites. Fees are currently advertised at $49 for one week of unlimited usage, $295 for six months of unlimited usage, $495 for one year of unlimited usage. Details available on their Web site.

Information about nonprofits

<http://www.human.com/inc>

This is the Internet Nonprofit Center, set up to be the home of donor and volunteer information on the Net. They say they have more info on nonprofits than any other site in the country.

<http://www.contact.org>

New site that contains a directory of nonprofit resources on the Web and links to over 5,000 nonprofit organizations, publications, and directories.

<http://www.cbbb.org/cbbb/pas.html>

Council of Better Business Bureaus' Philanthropic Advisory Service, with, among other things, reports on most-asked questions about charities and other soliciting organizations.

<http://www.give.org>

The National Charities Information Bureau site. Their mission is "to promote informed giving and charitable integrity, to enable more contributors to make sound giving decisions and to do all we can to encourage giving to charities that need and merit support. NCIB believes that donors are entitled to accurate information about the charitable organizations that seek their support. NCIB also believes that well-informed givers will ask questions and make judgments that will lead to an improved level of performance by charitable organizations."

<http://www.charityvillage.com/cvhome.html>

Charity Village. This site is devoted to the Canadian nonprofit sector, with enough international links to make it worth a look.

<http://www.charities.org/>

America's charities—example of a federated giving program that lists online info about the charities included under its umbrella.

Foundation and corporate giving sites

<http://www.cof.org>

The Council on Foundations

<http://www.cdinet.com/Benton/homepage.html>

Benton Foundation

<http://www.dana.org>

The Charles A. Dana Foundation

<http://www.ihf.org>

Irvine Health Foundation

<http://www.IBM.com/IBM/IBMGives>

IBM Corporate Philanthropy

<http://www.igc.org/kff>

Henry J. Kaiser Family Foundation

‹http://www.glef.org›

George Lucas Education Foundation

‹http://midas.org/mcf/mcf.html›

Marin Community Foundation

‹http://www.packfound.org/packhome.htm›

Packard Foundation

‹gopher://gopher.rwjf.org:4500›

Robert Wood Johnson Foundation

‹http://www.Sun.COM:80/corporateoverview/CorporateAffairs/ grants.html›

Sun Microsystems Foundation, Inc.

Miscellaneous sites for fundraisers

‹http://www.fv.com›

First Virtual Holdings, Inc. One example of how companies are trying to get around the security problems of the Internet and allow consumers (and donors) a safe way to transfer funds.

‹http://www.indepsec.org›

The Independent Sector is a coalition of foundation, corporate, and volunteer-based organizations with the mission to provide a national leadership forum to encourage philanthropy, volunteerism, and nonprofit initiatives. Stats on giving available from their site, as well as information on IS publications, projects, and members.

‹http://www.josseybass.com›

San Francisco publisher Jossey-Bass is known for publishing books that serve the nonprofit sector. You can find a catalog of those books, including ones for fundraisers, on their Web site.

<http://www.sec.gov/edgarhp.html>

EDGAR stands for Electronic Data Gathering, Analysis, and Retrieval system. It is the Security and Exchange Commission's database of corporate information, including all annual reports on Form 10-K or 10-KSB. Some fundraisers are looking here to get information about salaries and assets of corporate management.

<http://www.hoovers.com>

They bill themselves as "the ultimate source for company information." Some searching is free, but most of the really good stuff you have to pay for. For more information, drop by their Web site.

Martha Simpson is Director of Telecommunications Projects at the Support Center for Nonprofit Management, San Francisco. She compiled this listing in spring 1996. The material herein is copyright © 1996 by the Support Center for Nonprofit Management, 706 Mission Street, 5th Floor, San Francisco, California 94103-3113, phone (415) 541-9000, fax (415) 541-7708, World Wide Web: http://www.supportcenter.org/sf/ E-mail: Supportcenter@supportcenter.org

>>>

8

Cyber-fundraising

by ROBBIN ZEFF

Fundraising in cyberspace

Cyber-fundraising is the fundraising technique for the next millennium.
It is a new paradigm in fundraising where giving traditions need to be
developed among communities just now forming. The successful
fundraiser will be the one who artfully molds fundraising principles,
tactics, and techniques into the very heart of this new medium.

What are people in the nonprofit community saying about
cyber-fundraising? Beth Kanter of Arts Wire has found that their Web site
has resulted in "off-line" press such as *Internet World*. Moreover, funders
have seen their site and shown interest. Stephen Karnes of the Cenikor
Foundation has received some interest from potential donors because of
their Web site. And Howard Lake of City University in London says, "As a
fundraiser, I have benefitted from the resources I have uncovered and
listed on the (Web) site."

Cyber-fundraising is still in its infant, experimental stage. Its limits and true potential live in one's imagination and entrepreneurial spirit. Everything on the Internet is happening so quickly that today's infant ideas may become tomorrow's standard operating procedures. The public awareness element of maintaining a presence on the Internet grows in value as general access to the Internet expands. Without a doubt, public awareness and fundraising go hand-in-hand.

The giving community revisited

Philanthropic America is aging. The average direct mail donor is now a woman in her late sixties. The baby boomer generation is proving to have a tradition of giving, but the question remains as to whether Generation X will be able to pick up the slack. Moreover, the 1990s are showing a negligible increase in charitable giving, especially from foundation and corporate philanthropic giving programs.

The profile of the on-line community today is of Generation X (ages 16 to 34). It is yet to be seen which causes will inspire this generation to give. One thing is certain, this age group is part of the cyberspace revolution and they are dialing in and logging on-line. To reach Generation X where it listens and learns will pave the way to inspiring new donations.

As use of the Internet expands in society, the use of demographics will spread out in age, gender, and ethnic makeup. Thus, the Internet will quickly move from being a marketing tool that reaches only specific demographic groups, to becoming one of the top means of communicating with the general public.

In 1995, Americans contributed $143.9 billion to charities. According to *Giving USA* a report by American Association of Fund-Raising Counsel Trust for Philanthropy, these contributions came primarily from four communities and were divided as follows: individuals 80.8 percent, foundations 7.3 percent, bequests 6.8 percent, and corporations 5.1 percent. Close attention to these breakdowns will be key to developing a successful cyber-fundraising plan. Consequently, one can expect that the majority of contributions in cyberspace will be from individuals and will come in small dollar donations.

Cyber-fundraising will not replace other methods of fundraising. It is one more vehicle for reaching the giving community and should become a part of your organization's fundraising strategy. This chapter will look at each of the four broad giving communities (individual, foundations, corporate, and bequests) and the means by which your organization can reach them through your cyberspace fundraising efforts.

Electronic commerce

The true potential of cyber-fundraising will not be reached until commerce is readily exchanged electronically and the general public becomes secure regarding the exchange of commerce on-line.

Electronic payment methods are already in practice. Telephone sales, automatic teller machines, electronic fund transfers, and even electronic filing of income tax are now commonplace. What is new in cyberspace is the direct exchange of funds in sales transactions.

The benefit of using an electronic payment method is that one maintains a fluid progression from information request, interest in making a donation, to actually making the donation. In fundraising one never wants to lose entree to that "givable moment" when a donor is ready and willing to make a contribution. Electronic payment methods minimize the potential of a distraction occurring before payment is secured.

As growth in the volume of transactions corresponds to the commercialization of the Web, the risk of interception of a financial transaction mounts. Consequently, one of the keys to moving the Web from a marketing tool to a means for exchanging commerce is the development and acceptance of secure methods of payment.

Currently, there are two basic types of systems available for the exchange of commerce. One involves direct credit card usage and the other a separate ID number tied to a credit card. Both systems are transaction based.

>>> The first electronic commerce company to emerge was **First Virtual Holdings Inc.** [**<http://fv.com>**] of Cheyenne, Wyoming. Research conducted by First Virtual showed a higher comfort level with giving credit card information over the phone rather than electronically. Consequently, First Virtual designed a system where the part of the registration process that involves dispersing credit card information is done via an automated 800 number. When a

person signs up with First Virtual, he or she receives a First Virtual number that is used for Internet purchases. Each transaction is verified through an e-mail confirmation notice. When something is purchased, the buyer sends the merchant a First Virtual number. The buyer is then asked to confirm the transaction through an e-mail message. The First Virtual number works like a cyberspace-specific credit card that debits an already existing credit card.

>>> **Newtwatch [<http://www.cais.com/newtwatch/>]**, a political satire Web site on Speaker Newt Gingrich, was one of the first sites to use First Virtual as a means for accepting on-line contributions. Because Newtwatch is a political action committee, Federal Election Committee (FEC) regulations apply to all contributions. As a leader in the development of political Web pages, Matt Dorsey, founder and Webmaster of Newtwatch, requested and received an official FEC ruling on the acceptance of Internet political contributions.

>>> Most systems being developed for the exchange of electronic commerce, or more specifically electronic data interchange (EDI), are based on encryption. Encryption is a code system applied to a file to ensure the security of the transmitted information. To decode the encrypted message, the recipient needs the decoding key. In the case of a purchase, the identity of the person sending the message is available, but only the merchant's private decoding key can complete the transaction. We can expect in the near future that all buyers will have a personal digital signature to ensure authenticity.

>>> The first type of system puts a step between the buyer and seller with encryption to ensure security. **CyberCash [<http://www. cybercash.com>]** of Reston, Virginia, offers secured credit card transactions and will shortly provide debits through electronic card transactions. These electronic "cash" payment systems will act as trust accounts, where money is transferred into the trust account as needed and will allow for easy small dollar purchases.

>>> Many of the leaders in the on-line industry are actively engaged in partnerships with leading credit card companies and banks to develop safe and secure electronic payment systems. Without a

doubt, electronic commerce is the key to complete the commercialization of the Internet.

Individual contributors

Soliciting Membership

A Web site offers a nonprofit the perfect opportunity to attract persons navigating the Internet to the affairs and activities of the organization. The Internet community is extremely diverse and reaches a broad audience whose tastes, interests, and demographics are still unknown. A smartly designed Web site can attract individuals to the organization and promote membership, as well as solicit donations.

A membership form can be put directly on a Web site to facilitate easy enrollment. The form can ask the prospective member to input personal information in order to enlist in the nonprofit's activities and join as a member. When the form is completed the user can immediately be added to the organization's e-mail database and start receiving material from the organization within minutes.

Acquiring new members

Membership organizations need a steady influx of new members to balance the natural and inevitable membership attrition process. A Web site is a great way to gain new members, because the person accessing the site did so out of a personal need or interest. Specifically, the visitor found the organization's site rather than the organization seeking out the visitor. This puts the organization in the perfect situation to engage the visitor, either through an action step such as e-mailing a member of Congress, signing the guest book at the site, or by requesting the person join the organization.

Enhancing membership relations

The immediacy and ease of communication in cyberspace allows an organization to provide existing members with continual and timely updates of the organization's activities and programs. The closer a member feels to an organization, the more likely that person will participate in fundraising appeals.

Soliciting donations

Nonprofits will miss a great fundraising opportunity if a donor solicitation page is not included in an organization's Web site. The age-old saying in fundraising, "if you don't ask, you won't get" holds true in cyberspace as well.

The American Red Cross uses the Internet to alert interested persons about disasters and volunteering opportunities such as donating blood or making a financial contribution. Visitors to their Web site who want to help are asked to call an 800 number. The operator asks where the caller learned of the 800 number and keeps track of the original source of contact. This direct but low-pressure solicitation approach works well. The Red Cross has found that during an average month, calls to the 800-number initiated from a visit to their Web page surpasses television commercials and other media sources. Calls generated via the Web page have resulted in additional donations totaling from $5,000 to $10,000 in a month with either small or no disasters and considerably higher during peak disaster periods. For example in September 1995, the concern generated over Hurricane Marilyn resulted in close to $30,000 in donations from visitors to the Web page.

Payment methods

There are various payment methods being employed by nonprofit organizations for soliciting donations. The American Red Cross requests donors to call an 800-number where contributions are processed over the phone. The Ethiopian Jewry home page requests donors to mail in contributions and is receiving from 5 to 10 contributions a month via Internet interest. Majority '96, a political action committee, also requests donations be mailed but uses an interactive pledge button to automatically generate a pledge prompting e-mail message.

Special events

Organizations are experimenting with holding virtual fundraising events in cyberspace. Impact Online launched their **Cookin' on the Net** [<**http://www.cooknet.org/index.html#top**>] as a Web-based charity effort designed to raise money for nonprofit organizations helping to donate computer equipment and resources to disadvantaged children. Participants were asked to donate $12 electronically. In return, contributors received five recipes from renowned chefs in five cities: Boston, Chicago, New York, Los Angeles, and San Francisco. The event raised $1,500 in the first three weeks, although most contributions came through the mail, not electronically.

Another virtual event was held by Paranet titled **Cyberspace Challenge** [**\<http://cyberchallenge.paranet.com\>**] The event raised $10,000 for Big Brothers and Sisters. Cyberspace Challenge was a skills-based Internet competition for children. Most of the $10,000 was donated by corporate sponsors.

The commercial on-line services are also getting into the act by using cyberspace as a medium to increase business and help charities at the same time. America Online and PC Financial Network joined forces between December 15, 1995, and January 15, 1996, to raise money for Ronald McDonald Children's Charities. They jointly made donations for every on-line stock trade executed during that time period. The event raised over $84,000 and was hailed as a great success by all involved.

Advertising virtual events

How does one advertise virtual events? This is done by using all the outreach vehicles already at your disposal: mail, newsletters, and word of mouth as well as electronic mediums such as e-mail, newsgroups, and mailing lists on your Web site and announcements on other Web sites.

Advertising your event in cyberspace

Cyberspace can also be used to advertise a fundraising event. Philadelphia Aids Walk [**\<http://www.cortex.net/!!tUYilCSwWt UYilCSw/aidswalk/\>**] built a home page for their event. The **Jimmy V Celebrity Gold Classic** also has its own site [**\<http://jimmyv.org/ golfclassic.html\>**] where the organization not only advertises the event, but also solicits for sponsors by highlighting their sponsorship packages [\<http://jimmyv.org/sponsorship.html\>].

Fundraising products

The World Wide Web is also being used as a vehicle to advertise fundraising event products to the nonprofit community. On the Web you can find dozens of fundraising ideas for your next fundraising campaign: from selling candy [**\<http://www.moneymp.com\>**] to selling "make your own pizza" kits [**\<http://webcom.com/~pets/fundr/index.html\>**] and from selling seminars [**\<http://Fox.nstn.ca/~asi/\>**] to selling lottery-style scratch-off cards [**<http://www.transformation.com/scratch/>**] where the amount on the card is the amount the person should donate.

Major donor fundraising

The Internet is not known as the "toy" of the rich. It is not a place where the elite meet. The yacht club and the country club are still better avenues for mingling with the rich and famous. As is the case with most fundraising efforts, the majority of money to be made on the Internet will come in small dollar amounts. And yet the Internet can be a valuable tool in major donor prospect research. If you are conducting general background research, you can search newspaper and periodical databases from the *New York Times Fax* [**<http://www.nytimesfax.com>**] to the *San Jose Mercury News* [**<http://www.sjmercury.com/>**]. You can also look through *West's Legal Directory* for lawyers and law firms [**<http://www. wld.com/ldsearch.htm>**].

Prospect research companies such as **Waltman Associates** [**<http://www.umn.edu/nlhome/g248/bergq003/wa/>**] have compiled lists of Trustees of College and Universities, a Directory of Directors, and even made back issues of *Town & Country* magazine searchable for a fee. An indispensable tool for corporate research is Hoovers On-line which has a searchable directory of over 10,000 companies. There are also sites maintained by professional prospect researchers at public institutions such as **The Prospect Research Page** [**<http://weber.u.washington.edu/~ dlamb/research.html#corp>**] by David Lamb of the Development Office at the University of Washington that has links to a wide variety of valuable sites for prospect research.

There is even an Internet mailing list on prospect research called PRSPECT-L where professionals in the field exchange tips and tricks. To subscribe to this discussion group, e-mail a message to <Listserv@ bucknell.edu> with the following message: **subscribe prspct-l <firstname lastname>**. The discussion is archived and can be accessed through a gopher menu [**<gopher:///gopher.bucknell.edu:70/00/Services/ listserv/prspct-l/info>**].

Donor recognition

You can acknowledge and thank donors directly on your Web site. For example, on the home page for the **American Cancer Society**

[<http://www.cancer.org/>] acknowledgment is given for the support provided by the American Cancer Foundation in conjunction with Leo and Gloria Rosen for the development and maintenance of the site. Impact Online thanks its sponsors at the bottom of its home page [<http:///www.impactonline.org/>]

Direct mail in cyberspace

Like any community, the cyberspace community has developed an informal code of proper and improper behavior. For the cyberspace community, the location of activity is on the Internet and the code of conduct is called *netiquette.* A host of FAQs exist that discuss netiquette, most of which surrounds proper Usenet behavior. Netiquette becomes of central concern when one begins exploring the possibilities of direct mail via e-mail, newsgroups, mailing lists, and so on. Without a doubt, the answer to whether there will be advertising in cyberspace is no longer an "if" but a "how." And yet, utilizing the new media to facilitate direct mail techniques will require a thorough knowledge of netiquette as well as the new emerging cyberspace marketing paradigm.

The most obvious vehicle through which to do direct mail marketing is newsgroups, but that is strongly frowned upon in netiquette. One method used in direct marketing on the Internet has been given the pejorative term of *spam.* Spam is when a message is posted multiple times to a large number of newsgroups regardless of the subject of the newsgroup. The topic of the spam can be anything from an advertisement for hand cream to an alert about nuclear testing.

The term spam comes from a well known Monty Python sketch. In this sketch, a man is in a diner and asks the waitress what is on the menu. The waitress replies: "Well, there's egg and bacon; egg, sausage, and bacon; egg and spam; egg, bacon, and spam; egg, bacon, sausage, and spam; spam, bacon, sausage, spam, spam, spam, bacon, spam, tomato, and spam; spam, spam, spam, egg, and spam; spam, spam, spam, spam, spam, spam, baked beans, spam, spam, spam, and spam." The word spam is used in the waitress's reply repeatedly with no apparent meaning. Likewise, messages on the Internet that are out of context and considered virtual noise are considered spam.

The Internet community abhors spam; not only because it consists of inappropriate and out-of-context messages, but because it takes up space on the server. Multiple listings of the same message take up space and inspire large volumes of complaints in response to the spam. There is usually a 10 percent increase in newsgroup activity after the posting of a spam, and all this added activity can drain server space and resources.

Certain spam incidents are infamous in cyberspace. In 1994, the law firm of Canter and Siegel thought they had discovered the silver bullet for tapping the Internet as a cheap marketing medium and posted an advertisement for green card assistance to over 7,000 newsgroups. Canter and Siegel received few requests for green card assistance but the response by the Internet community was fast and swift. The server that Canter and Siegel used, Internet Direct, crashed fifteen times under the flood of thirty thousand hate mail messages and flames (argumentative messages) received in just eighteen hours. Internet Direct stopped the Canter and Siegel account.

A *flame* is an offensive or unmannerly e-mail originated in the Usenet environment. Flaming is the process whereby one user sends another an acerbic, offensive, or unmannerly e-mail. The instigation of a flame is usually an inappropriate comment or basic breach of netiquette by a veteran newsgroup user. Mistakes made by novice users rarely result in flaming. A new user is allowed much more latitude than is a long-time practitioner. Flames should be used in moderation. For those partial to flaming, there are now newsgroups dedicated to this art.

Canter and Siegel then took several steps. First they threatened to sue Internet Direct for $250,000 for loss of business. Then Canter and Siegel set up accounts on two other providers promising even more advertisements. The Internet community went wild in response. Even though Canter and Siegel received tremendous press coverage, they were blacklisted from the Internet community, with service providers choosing to drop the Canter–Siegel accounts rather than face the rampage of the Internet community.

Robert Raisch, Vice-Chairperson of the Internet Business Association and founder of The Internet Company, calls spam advertisements postage-due marketing. Raisch defines postage-due marketing as, "using the global Internet as a direct marketing vehicle to distribute messages to users with little concern for their topical appropriateness or the costs involved in their distribution." In using this type of marketing, the advertiser forces the consumer to bear part of the costs of distribution, whether the consumer is interested in the product or not. This could be likened to a telemarketer calling collect. Newsgroup participants do not want their discussion disrupted with advertisements. In response, special advertising-friendly newsgroups have been developed to deter such subject noise from cluttering up the legitimate discussion in a newsgroup.

Commercialization of the Internet is definitely here to stay. The lesson to be learned from the Canter and Siegel spam war is that advertising on the Internet is not inherently bad. Rather, advertisers need to follow proper netiquette—that is, in the appropriate locations and not through unsolicited e-mail or newsgroup advertising where the recipient is forced to read and pay for unsolicited and unwanted messages.

As with any community, cyberspace has developed internal means to punish those that break the rules. In terms of newsgroup advertising, blacklists such as the **Blacklist of Internet Advertisers [<http://math-www.uni-paderborn.de/~axel/BL/blacklist.html>**] have developed that document spam incidents. Moreover, when you have a burgeoning new community, the last thing your nonprofit wants is to acquire a negative image. The results of improper netiquette are that people would not visit and might even boycott your site, directories will not list your organization, and hackers might even sabotage the site (this translates into time, if not monetary expense, to repair the damage). At the extreme, the negative cyber-image translated into the general public arena tarnishes an organization's good name.

The debate on this issue is far from over. The September 29, 1995, edition of *The Friday Report* published by Hoke Communications, reported that Marketry, Inc. a mailing list company in Bellevue, Washington was handling the product "E-Mail Internet Interest Selector" that had a list of 250,000 e-mail addresses. By November, Marketry, Inc. had dropped the product. One of the main reasons given for this was the lack of technology for allowing e-mail addresses to opt out of receiving e-mail advertisements presented to the company by the Internet community. The product was bought by **DM Group** of Aurora, Ohio [**<http://www.dm1.com/>**].

This begs the question, how can one successfully carry out direct mail in cyberspace? First of all, an organization needs to develop its own e-mail database and not take the apparently easy route of using an existing listserv or newsgroup. The old saying "if it looks too good to be true, it probably is" holds true in cyberspace as well. Moreover, in developing the e-mail database, the organization should first let the user know that the organization might sell their e-mail database as a way to raise funds, and that everyone who participates in the database is aiding in the fundraising process. The user should then be given the opportunity to opt out of receiving solicitations by e-mail. With present mail list technology, this is not easily doable; however, as e-mail databases are built via Web sites, this option can be included.

Inevitably people's e-mail addresses will be as pervasive as their phone and fax numbers and as accessible to direct marketers. E-mail will be the appropriate place for solicitations—*not* a spam to unrelated or inappropriate newsgroups.

How will a virtual direct mail appeal look? E-mail tends to be short and to the point. Undoubtedly, direct mail via e-mail will follow the same style, but with the added advantage of inviting the recipient to visit the organization's Web site for a more multimedia presentation of the appeal. Moreover, when sending out e-mail solicitations, an identifying marker in the subject heading would be appropriate in order to identify the message as a solicitation.

Sale of publications and other material

Nonprofits have found that selling related items can be a profitable addition to budget enrichment. The Sierra Club, one of the founders of nonprofits selling merchandise to supplement their income, has their full catalogue of books available to the Internet community [**<http://www. sierraclub.org/books/>**]. Whether one is selling publications or T-shirts, your Web site is a direct outlet for sales, and has the potential to reach a broader audience than does the mailing of catalogues alone; the Internet reaches millions worldwide. This is also an inexpensive way to continue advertising products after a new product line has been introduced.

Order forms on-line allow purchases to happen immediately by using an electronic payment method. Also, featuring products on-line one can present a full-color graphic of the item without the extravagant costs of full-color advertisement in traditional print media. For example, the Amnesty International publication page displays its full line of merchandise, from publications to T-shirts. The customer can choose to print either a page or the entire catalogue in full graphics or in a text only version.

Foundation fundraising on the Internet

Foundation prospect research

Information on foundations can be found in three types of sites. The first are the sites of key foundation assistance and resource centers, both on a national and state-wide basis. For example, the **Foundation Center** has a Web site [**<http://www.fndcenter.org/>**] that includes information on the grant-writing process, current and past issues of their newsletter *Philanthropy News Digest,* as well as links to foundation home pages categorized by type of foundation. The **Council on Foundations'** home page [**<http:///www.cof.org/>**] links to other foundation home pages, but only those that belong to the Council. On the state level, one can also find directory listings of foundations. For example, the Northern California Community Foundation, Inc.'s site **Foundations On-Line** [**<http://www. foundations.org/>**] includes links to foundations and grantmakers, as well as fundraising software, fundraising consultants and fundraising products.

The second type of site consists of foundation Web sites. The number of foundations with a presence on the Web is growing every month. As of this printing there are over 50 foundations whose Web pages provide various levels of information. Some are merely Web presentations from the text of the organizational brochure with no links to additional pages of information. Other foundation sites provide a complete introduction to the foundation, its mission, funding priorities, grant guidelines, grant recipients, and information on the staff. Since modification of Web material is much easier and more cost effective than reprinting and disseminating a brochure, material on foundations can be kept up to date more readily.

And third, commercial sites are appearing that offer access to fee-based searchable foundation databases. **Access Point Fundraising System** debuted in 1996 with a keyword searchable database for foundations and another for corporate giving [**<http//www.accesspt.com/fundsys/ fundsys.html>**].

Applying for grants

In the near future, one can expect more and more foundations to accept applications over the Internet. The process could take on various forms. The first step will probably be that foundations accept grant applications as transferred files, minimizing the copying and postage costs for grantees.

Another future option is to supply the grant application on an on-line form, where the grantee fills out and submits the application on-line. In this way, a uniform standard would be maintained to allow instant submission of an application.

Finally, in the future, grant writing on the Internet could follow the virtual document model where a grant application is a combination of text, graphics, and links. This interactive and multimedia grant application would provide the program officer with a broader access to the grantee's work. For example, a grantee could demonstrate success as a technical assistance provider by providing links to the organizations she or he assist. Other multimedia dimensions could consists of 15- to 30-second video or audio clips demonstrating the work of the nonprofit. This type of a virtual document also could be employed for the grant recipient's reporting requirements.

Foundations are also investigating how to assist their grantees in jumping on the Internet: What would be the best resources and assistance they could provide to facilitate this move? For example, Pfizer is in the early stages of developing a program to assist a group of current grantees to gain presence on the Internet. The program provides funding for equipment, technical assistance on Web design, and maintenance. Paula Luff, Manager of Corporate Philanthropy Programs, sees this program as providing their grantees with valuable access to a variety of tools for disseminating and gathering information. Moreover, Paula feels confident that a Web presence will help their grantees "acquire and maintain member relationships as well as expand the organization's donor base."

Corporate fundraising

Prospect research

The Internet holds a wealth of material for corporate prospect researching. As previously mentioned, there are Web sites by prospect research companies who offer services through their home page for a fee, and directories of prospect research resources put together by university development offices. Another equally valuable resource is to examine a company's Web site. In corporate research, one can learn about the top officers and management at a company site. Many companies include biographies of management on their Web site, some with photographs and audio tracks [<http://www.ibm.com/Finding/Welcome/>].

If one is planning to approach a company for a donation, whether through the company's philanthropic giving program or in a cause-related marketing capacity through the marketing department, a good knowledge of corporate priorities is always valuable. For example, the **AMD** Web page [**<http://www.amd.com/img/imagemap/shmap.conf?268,9>**] not only provides background about the company, the corporate mission statement, and press releases, but also discusses their target markets. Gathering this material used to require a great deal of research, now it is available all in one place. Acquiring this kind of inside material before meeting with a company is invaluable.

Corporate partnerships—cause-related marketing

One of the greatest challenges on the Web right now is getting people to look at your home page. With 100,000 plus home pages on the Web, the nonprofit needs to develop ways to lead interested persons to its page. Hyperlinks with similar nonprofits is one way, but in terms of fund-raising, there is another possibility. In cause-related marketing, a company tries to link itself with a nonprofit organization in order to boost its image and sales and at the same time raise money for the organization. Cyber-fundraising offers great potential for corporate and nonprofit partnerships.

The benefits of cause-related marketing to the company and nonprofit alike are now extending into cyberspace. For example, **Rhino Chasers** micro beer, a product of William & Scott Brewing Company of California, [**<http://www.rhinochasers.com>**] has had a relationship with the African Wildlife Foundation (AWF) for two and a half years. The company decided to get involved in a cause-related marketing campaign because the demographics for micro beer drinkers are men and women between the ages of 25 and 35. This group is known to respond well to cause-related marketing through the good works for charity by such industry leaders as the Body Shop, Starbucks Coffee, and Ben and Jerry's Ice Cream.

The makers of Rhino Chasers decided to find a nonprofit to associate with that would tie into its name. The product name of Rhino Chasers came from a surfing term, but its association with the rhino lead to its partnership with AWF. Rhino Chasers gives a percentage of its profits to AWF. In addition, Rhino Chasers helps publicize the work of AWF by putting the AWF logo on their beer bottle labels and including AWF brochures in Rhino Chaser mailings. As Tim Pai, CFO of Rhino Chasers points out, "From day one we've done our best to promote AWF." When

Rhino Chasers decided to put up a Web page, they told AWF that just as they publicize AWF everywhere else, their Web page would include a link to an AWF page as well—and Rhino Chasers would be happy to design the page.

Leigh Bailey, Development Associate at AWF, decided to take on the Web page assignment both in terms of content and design. Even though AWF's computer system was still DOS based, Leigh worked on the Web page at home using her PC and her personal Internet account. Leigh taught herself HTML and calculates that it took about 10 hours total to design the page, type in the text, and learn HTML. "I think people can do Web pages themselves," says Leigh.

"In designing the pages I tried to keep it graphically simple because most computers can't pick up large images. I also tried to mimic our colors and still have colors that would look good on the Web. And finally, I tried to keep the language simple.

"The contents of the page include an introduction to AWF with links to pages on the rhino and the elephant. In the future we want to include highlights from our newsletter as the changing element of the page. Other future links include news from Africa as well as links to African and wildlife pages."

AWF plans to raise funds through their page. The first generation of the Web site will not use an electronic payment system due to concerns about the safety of electronic payment transactions at this time. Instead, Leigh points out, "We'll have our address, phone number, and e-mail."

The connection between Rhino Chasers and AWF has been beneficial to both parties. For Rhino Chasers, this association with AWF is another way for them to stand out in the crowd of other micro brews. Also, both are benefitting from exposure to the other's base: Rhino Chaser's demographics (25 to 35) is quite different from AWF's demographics (older and more established society folks). This cross-fertilization holds great promise.

The Web site had an added benefit for AWF. When Leigh presented the Web site to the AWF board, they were most enthusiastic about the job Leigh had done on her own initiative. The board is now working with the staff to upgrade the organization's entire computer system, so that all staff in the organization can go on-line from their desks.

The Rhino Chasers and AWF is just one type of partnership arrangement. Other potential partnership arrangements could be between nonprofits and electronic commerce providers. For example, the provider could advertise that every time someone signs up for or uses their service, a donation would be made to the nonprofit. If the nonprofit has a large e-mail database and membership base with demonstrable loyalty of members, associating with the nonprofit could boost the provider's market share with significant sales increases.

Memorials

The Internet is still too new a fundraising technique to be the focal point in bequests, but there are a host of memorials springing up on the Internet. In fundraising, many contributions are given in honor of loved ones who have passed away. This is particularly true for health-related organizations that deal with the funding of research for specific diseases such as cancer and aids. Sites of this nature can facilitate memorial contributions by providing a Web site vehicle on which to make a direct donation in a loved one's honor. Also, as memorials and virtual memorial gardens spring up on the Web, a nonprofit could develop partnership links with these sites. Unlike memorials of old where a name alone was placed on a plaque or a page in a program, a Web memorial could include pictures as well as text remembering that person's commitment to a cause or an organization's mission. For example, immediately after the death of Jerry Garcia of the rock band Grateful Dead, pages memorializing Jerry Garcia and offering a place for people to grieve appeared on the Web. On the site **In Memoriam—Jerry Garcia** [**<http://hake.com/gordon/garcia.html>**], a request is made on behalf of Deborah Koons Garcia that donations in honor of Jerry be sent to either the Haight Ashbury Free Clinic–Detox Unit or the Rex Foundation.

Saving money is raising money

Another way of looking at raising money in cyberspace is by saving money. Cyberspace offers the nonprofit a myriad means by which to save money in postage and printing, as well as in payment for services. In other words, your organization will be able to respond to requests for information without incurring the cost of postage and without generating extra paper.

A Web site is a perfect location to tell and sell your organization on a budget.

As already mentioned in other sections of this book, your Web site will help you save money in the following ways:

>>> E-mailing messages to staff, volunteers, members, and interested persons as well as responding to requests for assistance.

>>> Advertising and finding volunteers.

>>> Posting publications and newsletters.

Without a doubt, the Web provides a wealth of opportunities for the nonprofit community to be creative as it taps the giving potential of the cyberspace community. New fundraising tactics and techniques will be developed as we blend the Web into our organization's overall marketing mix.

>>>

9

Glossary of Internet terms

by MICHAEL STEIN

Autoreply

An autoreply is an automatic e-mail tool with its own Internet e-mail address. You set up an autoreply with your Internet Service Provider. When someone sends e-mail to the autoreply, it will automatically send back an electronic document containing information you maintain. You should receive a regular activity log of "hits" to your autoreply. It is a useful way to make information available with a minimum amount of human intervention.

Browser

A browser is a computer software program used with an Internet account to allow viewing of text, images, and other media on the Internet. The term is most commonly used to refer to graphical World Wide Web software such as Netscape's Navigator and Microsoft's Internet Explorer. It can also refer to non-graphical browsers such as "Lynx," which is a text-only browser that can be used at modem speeds as low as 2400 baud.

Chat

Chat is a generic term referring to any sort of "live" communication on the Internet or one of the online services, where two or more users are simultaneously connected and talking to each other with their keyboards. Chatting is one of the most popular activities on America Online and CompuServe, two commercial online services. Chatting also takes places on the Internet itself, and it is soon anticipated on the World Wide Web.

Electronic mail or e-mail

Electronic mail (or e-mail) is the most commonly used tool on the Internet today. It allows you to send and receive electronic messages with anyone else on the Internet. Many offices have internal e-mail distributed over their own networks, which may or may not be able to exchange messages through the Internet.

FTP

FTP stands for File Transfer Protocol and is a storage and file transfer standard on the Internet. An FTP archive is a library storage place for electronic documents. FTP is also a software program used with an Internet account to retrieve files from FTP archives.

Gopher

A Gopher is a text-based Internet tool for storage and retrieval of files and documents. Gophers were the predecessors of Web sites, allowing individuals worldwide to retrieve information over the Internet. Gophers were particularly popular at universities, which used them to disseminate information about academic and research subjects. Gophers were the first Internet tools that led to the development of Internet-wide search engines, known under the acronym "Veronica." Gophers are still in use today, but have been overshadowed by Web sites.

Home page

A home page is a term commonly used to describe a "graphical World Wide Web site" on the Internet. For example: "We have a home page on the Web now." See *World Wide Web*.

Infobot

A technical term used interchangeably with "autoreply." It is a shortened form of "information robot." See *autoreply*.

Internet

The Internet is the backbone of high-speed phone and data lines that crisscross the globe and allow computer users with the appropriate software to send and receive messages, and browse information and data resources. Access to the Internet requires an account with an Internet provider. Thousands of commercial Internet Service Providers (and several nonprofits), as well as online services like America Online, sell access to the Internet to over 15 million Americans. Universities also provide Internet access.

Internet Service Provider (ISP)

An ISP provides access to the Internet via dial-up phone lines, usually for a monthly fee. ISPs include GNN, Netcom, Hooked, and the Institute for Global Communications.

Java

An evolving technology on the World Wide Web that allows images and graphics to be "animated." Java animations can only be viewed by Web software browsers that support the Java language. Current releases of Netscape and Microsoft browsers now support basic Java animations.

Listserv

See *mailing list*.

Lynx

See *browser*.

Mailing list

"Listserv" and "mailing list" means any type of Internet discussion group where people congregate to discuss issues and exchange information. A mailing list is a "group" of e-mail accounts that are tied together through a central e-mail address. Each mailing list has a theme or subject and people will "join" this mailing list and expect to participate in discussion or information exchange about a particular theme or subject.

Netscape

A commercial Internet company that manufactures and distributes the popular "Navigator" graphical Web browser. New releases of Netscape products are available free from the Netscape home page at <http://www.netscape.com>.

Online

Being on the Internet is being on-line. You're also online if you log onto an online service even if you don't access the Internet.

Plug-in

A Plug-in is a software program that accompanies a graphical Web browser to allow the user to view specialty multimedia productions that are part of Web sites. Many plug-ins can be downloaded free from the Internet. Also see *shockwave* and *RealAudio*.

RealAudio

Real Audio is a Web browser plug-in that allows a user to listen to audio files that are part of Web sites. RealAudio, a trademarked product made by Progressive Networks in Seattle, is distributed free over the Internet. RealAudio revolutionized audio on the Internet by allowing audio files to begin playing "instantly" (without lengthy downloads), while the rest of the file is downloaded as a "backstream" and fed progressively into the audio player. Similar technology will soon arrive for Internet video.

Server push

A server push is a feature on a Web site that allows multiple graphic images to be sequentially "staggered" or "pushed" at a viewer. For an example, see the Rainforest Action Network home page at <http://www.ran.org>.

Shockwave

Shockwave is a Web browser plug-in that allows a user to view full-motion animated images and graphics that are part of Web sites. Shockwave animations are created with Macromedia Director software.

URL

URL stands for Uniform Resource Locator, and is a technical standard for the addressing of resources on the Internet. <http://www.nrdc.org> is the URL for the Natural Resources Defense Council Web home page. An FTP site would be addressed as <ftp://ftp.igc.org>, and a Gopher would be addressed as <gopher://gopher.igc.apc.org>.

Web

Short for World Wide Web. See *World Wide Web*.

Webweaver

A person who builds and maintains Web sites. Used interchangeably with "Webmaster."

World Wide Web

A standard for the exchange of text, images, sounds, and audio on the Internet. The Web is accessed with a browser that is capable of displaying what is available on a Web site. The Web is organized into "home pages" where individuals and organizations assemble material for public viewing. Also see *browser* and *URL*.

Yahoo!

A popular Web search engine which allows users to search for information on Web sites. Over 8 million people access Yahoo! daily. It can be accessed at <http://www.yahoo.com>.

>>>

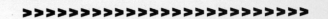

About the principal contributors to this book

Nick Allen

Nick Allen is a senior consultant at Mal Warwick & Associates. He directs the firm's Internet fundraising program, helping nonprofits use the Internet to raise money, build stronger donor relationships, activate members, and influence people. Nick has 25 years experience in building nonprofit organizations. He has worked as executive director (and founder) of Neighbor to Neighbor; Washington director of the Fenton Communications public interest PR firm; and president of Action Response, which developed rapid response systems using phone, fax, and Internet services. E-mail: <nick@malwarwick.com>, phone: (510) 843-8888.

Michael Johnston

Michael Johnston, the president of Hewitt and Johnston Consultants (Toronto), first gained fundraising experience as a senior consultant and director with Stephen Thomas Associates, one of the first fundraising firms in Canada to work exclusively with nonprofit organizations. Over his 10 years in the business, Mike has worked with hundreds of nonprofit organizations in Canada, the U.S., and the U.K.—including the Red Cross Society, Greenpeace, and Amnesty International. His work has also taken him to Australia as a fundraising consultant for the Labour Party. E-mail: <hjc@io.org>, phone (416) 588-7780.

Michael Stein

Michael Stein, special projects director of the Institute for Global Communications (IGC), is a pioneer in helping nonprofits use the Internet effectively. As a senior IGC staff member for five years, he's helped nonprofits create their Internet strategies, develop their Web pages, and figure out how to make the many new Internet tools work for their organizations. Michael is the author (with Gary Wolf) of *Aether Madness: An Offbeat Guide to the Online World*, published by Peachpit Press in December 1994. Michael has also worked for the National Toxics Campaign Fund, the Pesticide Action Network, the Environmental Support Center, Apple Computer Community Affairs, and the Right-to-Know Computer Network (RTK-NET). E-mail: <mstein@igc.org>, phone: (415) 561-6100.

Mal Warwick

Mal Warwick is chairman of Mal Warwick & Associates, Inc., a Berkeley, California-based fundraising and marketing firm. He is also vice-chair (and co-founder) of the Share Group, a nationwide telephone fundraising and outreach company. His seven previous books on fundraising include the classic *How to Write Successful Fundraising Letters* and *The Hands-On Guide to Fundraising Strategy & Evaluation*. Mal's clients have included many of the nation's leading charitable causes and institutions as well as five Democratic Presidential campaigns and hundreds of other organizations. He and his colleagues at Mal Warwick & Associates have raised an estimated $300 million since the firm's founding in 1979. E-mail: <mal@malwarwick.com>, phone: (510) 843-8888.

Robbin Zeff

Robbin Zeff is president of the Zeff Group, a consulting firm specializing in strategic Internet planning and training for nonprofit organizations and businesses. Considered one of the leaders in the emerging field of Cyber-Fundraising, her clients span the spectrum from small grassroots groups to national associations. Robbin's new book, *The Nonprofit Guide to the Internet,* will be available in the fall of 1996 from John Wiley & Sons. Her article "Navigating the Internet for Nonprofits" appeared in the 1996 edition of *The Nonprofit Management Handbook.* An experienced fundraiser and trainer, Robbin has conducted seminars and spoken at conferences worldwide.

>>>

About the organizations behind this book

Mal Warwick & Associates

Mal Warwick & Associates, Inc. is a fundraising and marketing company with a staff of 18. Since its founding in Berkeley in 1979, the firm has served hundreds of nonprofit causes and institutions all across North America, including many of the world's leading charities, scores of local and regional organizations, and five Democratic Presidential campaigns. Over the years, the firm has been responsible for raising an estimated $300 million.

Mal Warwick & Associates' services include:

>>> marketing campaigns for organizations and ideas

>>> full-service direct mail fundraising

>>> membership development and fundraising on the Internet

>>> consulting by the project, by the month, or by the day

>>> copywriting and design of letters, brochures, newsletters, annual reports

>>> Mal Warwick's EditExpress℠ for fast turnaround editing

>>> development audits

>>> marketing and fundraising videos

Additional services are available from two affiliated companies:

>>> *Response Management Technologies, Inc.* (Berkeley) offers data processing, donor file maintenance, donor acknowledgments, fundraising analysis, and laser-printing services.

>>> *The Share Group, Inc.,* headquartered in Somerville, Massachusetts, serves progressive nonprofit organizations and political campaigns and socially responsible businesses with a wide range of telemarketing services. Among these are telefundraising and grassroots lobbying campaigns, opinion research facilities, customer service, and other commercial services. Share operates calling centers in Somerville and Hadley, Massachusetts, Washington, D.C., and San Francisco.

How to contact Mal Warwick & Associates:

Mal Warwick & Associates, Inc.
2550 Ninth Street
Suite 103
Berkeley, California 94710-2516
Phone (510) 843-8888
Toll-free (888) 225-5625
Fax (510) 843-0142
E-mail <info@malwarwick.com>

The Institute for Global Communications

The Institute for Global Communications (IGC) is the nation's largest nonprofit provider of Internet and World Wide Web services. With over 45 staff members, IGC serves a unique niche of progressive nonprofit organizations.

IGC has 10 years of experience making the Internet work for activist organizations and individuals. IGC is home to five major online communities: EcoNet, PeaceNet, ConflictNet, LaborNet, and WomensNet. IGC serves over 15,000 members, including Amnesty International, Rainforest Action Network, Pesticide Action Network, Center for Third World Organizing, Teamsters Union, National Employment Lawyers Association, Human Rights Watch, Sierra Club, and UNICEF.

IGC has built and maintains its own Internet infrastructure with a state-of-the-art server based in Menlo Park, California, and is thus able to offer Internet ramp services to all its members (SLIP and PPP). Individual members pay an average of $12.50 per month to maintain accounts, receive and send e-mail, participate in conference forums, and surf the World Wide Web. Organizational members purchase group accounts for $3.50 per month.

IGC distributes its own fully integrated Internet navigation software package for $25 which includes the latest release versions of Netscape Navigator (Web browser) and Eudora (electronic mail).

In addition to Internet ramp services, IGC also offers a complete selection of specialty Internet products and services. World Wide Web hosting tops this list of services, and IGC now hosts over 400 Web sites for progressive nonprofit organizations. Other products include Domain Name Service registration, Majordomo Internet mailing lists, Gopher and FTP sites, and Automatic Reply e-mail tools. Internet consulting rounds off the services of IGC. IGC helps nonprofits with strategic Internet planning, training, Web building and upkeep, and content development.

Another critical aspect of IGC's work is its strategic partnership programs with organizations and networks. IGC's Outreach staff come from a variety of backgrounds within the environmental, human rights, labor, women's, and conflict resolution movements. Through program and project partnerships, IGC helps to build grassroots activist work.

Some of IGC's current programs include: Environmental Justice Networking Project, African American Networking Project, and Asian Community Online Network. IGC staff meet with movement activists, attend meetings and events, and develop staffed and funded projects.

IGC was founded in 1986. Its headquarters are located in the Thoreau Center for Sustainability in the Presidio of San Francisco, a former military base recently converted into a national park. IGC also maintains an office in Washington, D.C.

IGC is a project of the Tides Center, also a Thoreau Center resident, and the organization that fueled the creation of the Thoreau Center.

How to contact IGC:

Institute for Global Communications
Presidio Building 1012, First Floor
Torney Avenue
P.O. Box 29904
San Francisco, California 94129-0904
Phone (415) 561-6100
Fax (415) 561-6101
Automatic information reply: <igc-info@igc.org>
Web <http://www.igc.org>
Email <outreach@igc.org>

>>>

How this book was produced

Fundraising on the Internet is a great example of the growing role that computer technology in general—and the Internet in particular—is coming to play in publishing.

For starters, this project matured from a vague outline into a finished book in less than two weeks. The subject matter aside, it would never have occurred to us to compile a book of this sort under such a brutal schedule even two or three years ago. For example:

>>> Working from our homes and offices (usually in different cities) in the San Francisco Bay area, we used e-mail over the Internet to exchange messages and receive draft text and graphics from our collaborators in Toronto, New York, and San Francisco.

>>> Robbin Zeff's contribution—what we've termed Chapter 8—is, as you can readily see, reproduced directly from the page proofs of her forthcoming book. This material arrived from John Wiley & Sons almost literally at the last minute—too late for us to reformat in our own style.

>>> We used several computers in assembling this book. But the lion's share of the production work took place on my laptop, sometimes through the docking stations I have installed at home and at my office—and sometimes (right now, for example) on my lap in an irresistibly comfortable armchair.

>>> The workhorse software used in creating this book was garden-variety, off-the-shelf WordPerfect 6.1 for Windows running on Windows 95. I accessed the Internet via CompuServe's Mosaic browser and captured screen images using a $29.95 graphics conversion program Nick picked up at CompUSA. Nothing fancy!

>>> Nick wrote and edited mostly in Microsoft Word and used Netscape to access the Web. We communicated largely via IGC's e-mail network. However, we frequently exchanged text as "binary" files between our CompuServe accounts, which permitted us to preserve the files' formatting and typography.

>>> The body text was set in 12-point ITC Garamond, headlines in Futura Extra Bold. With the exception of the direct mail examples reproduced in these pages (which were merely "pasted up" in a distressingly old-fashioned way), the "artwork" was produced on a Lexmark Optra R printer at 600 or 1200 dpi.

If any of this sounds like whiz-bang, state-of-the-art technology, rest assured that it isn't. My laptop and printer are on the expensive end of the spectrum but readily available off-the-shelf. The rest is downright old-fashioned. In fact, I'm quite confident that the techno-nerds among my readers are now snickering loudly at the primitive tools at my disposal. ("Cheeez!—This guy uses CompuServe Mosaic to get on the Net?!")

Now you know.

—M.W.